THIS IS
ROCKET
SCIENCE

An Activity Guide

THIS IS
ROCKET
SCIENCE

An Activity Guide

70 Fun and Easy Experiments for Kids to Learn
More About Our Solar System

EMMA VANSTONE

founder of Science Sparks

PAGE STREET
PUBLISHING CO.

PAGE STREET
PUBLISHING CO.

First published in 2018 by

Page Street Publishing Co.

27 Congress Street, Suite 105

Salem, MA 01970

www.pagestreetpublishing.com

Distributed by Macmillan, sales in Canada by The Canadian Manda Group.

22 21 20 19 18   1 2 3 4 5

ISBN-13: 978-1-62414-524-7

ISBN-10: 1-62414-524-8

Library of Congress Control Number: 2017961189

Cover and book design by Page Street Publishing Co.

Photography by Charlotte Dart

Printed and bound in the United States

TO ZAK, SYDNEY, HANNAH AND
CHARLIE, WHO INSPIRE ME EVERY DAY.

☆ ☆ ☆

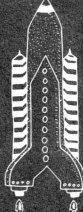

INTRODUCTION

"It's not rocket science," an often-used phrase, implies that rocket science is very difficult, which, of course it is. Getting spacecraft into space is an incredible feat of engineering and science, but the underlying principles (which are explored through the 70 activities in this book) are actually quite simple.

It takes a massive amount of power to launch a spacecraft into space. For example, it has to overcome gravity, cope with the many hazards of space and then survive a bumpy return back through the Earth's atmosphere without falling apart from the huge amount of heat and friction generated.

This Is Rocket Science: An Activity Guide explores the forces experienced by a spacecraft as it travels into space and back to Earth.

In this book you will find out how to make bottle, cork and film canister rockets, reduce the slowing effects of friction and air resistance, use air resistance to slow a fall, discover some of the difficulties encountered by astronauts in space and tour the solar system, taking note of the unimaginable distances involved and features of each planet.

Have a flick through: be inspired, go create, have fun and learn at the same time. You'll soon be reading Sir Isaac Newton's Laws of Motion and thinking how much sense they make and how you can relate them to everyday life.

Have you ever let a balloon go before tying it up and watched it fly around the room? That's a great demonstration of Newton's Third Law. Air rushes out of the balloon and the opposite reaction is that the balloon flies upwards. In the case of a rocket, it's the force of hot gases rushing downwards out of the engine's exhausts that creates an opposite upward force, pushing the rocket off the ground. Think how heavy a rocket is and how much thrust there needs to be for it accelerate upwards at the speeds needed to overcome gravity . . . It really is incredible.

Scientists observe, measure and communicate their findings with others, just like you're going to do with these projects. When you measure something, think about the best way to do it: Should you use a ruler or do you need something much bigger? The solar system is so big we have to scale it down; something you'll find out about in this book. When you've done one activity, try to predict what will happen if you change a variable. For example, if you make a film canister rocket using half a canister of water, can you predict what would happen if you used a full canister of water? When you've finished an activity, think about how to communicate your findings—could you make a mini video presentation?

The activities in this book are all stand-alone, so don't feel you need to do them in order, and if something doesn't work right away, just tweak the design a little and try again. Take some time and enjoy the journey to space and back.

All scientists take notes, record data, draw pictures, take photos and track progress. Your first task is to create your own personalized Space Passport to record your journey.

CREATE A SPACE PASSPORT

Rocket science takes you into space, around the solar system and back home to Earth. Can you create and keep a journal documenting your journey? Include chapters for the rocket launch, life in space, your trip to each planet and safe landing on Earth.

☆ Notebook

☆ Pens and pencils

Try to include lots of different methods of recording data in your Space Passport. You could draw sketches and diagrams, design tables and graphs or write diary entries of your findings and add photos.

GLORIOUS GRAVITY

Have you ever wondered why you don't shoot off into space when you jump; how a rocket gets off the ground; or why a toy car rolling down a ramp moves faster than on flat surface? To understand all of these things, you need to learn about forces.

Forces are all around us all the time. One big force is gravity. Gravity pulls objects towards the Earth; it's the reason we walk on the ground and don't float around, and why planes and rockets need engines to lift into the air. Gravity not only keeps us on Earth, it also keeps the Earth and other planets revolving around the Sun.

Gravity is a big issue when it comes to rocket science, because to get into space, a rocket needs to escape the gravitational force trying to pull it back to Earth. A rocket is able to launch and accelerate as long as the thrust force upwards is greater than the gravity and drag which slow it down.

Imagine life with no gravity: We'd have to be tethered to the Earth to stop us from floating away, and the atmosphere, rivers and oceans would all drift off into space!

GRAVITY SPLAT

✬ SCIENTIFIC CONCEPT—GRAVITY

Have you ever wondered why things fall to the ground when you drop them; why we don't all float around above the ground; or why astronauts can jump much higher on the Moon than on Earth? It's all because of a pulling force called gravity.

Bigger objects have a greater gravitational force. The Moon is much smaller than the Earth and so has much weaker gravity. The Moon's gravity is about one-sixth of that on Earth, which is why you can jump higher there.

✬ Large piece of white paper/white sheet/cardboard

✬ Small water balloons

✬ Funnel

✬ Water-based, non-toxic paint

✬ Water

Pick an area outside that can be paint splattered (ask an adult first!), and lay down the paper or sheet.

To make the paint balloons, blow up the balloon, let the air out and then place a small funnel into the top of the balloon. Pour in a good amount of paint before filling with water from the tap and tying the balloon end securely. Give your balloon a good shake to mix the water and paint. The water helps stretch the balloon so it will break more easily.

Once you've made a few balloons, think about how to test them. What do you think will happen when you drop the balloons? You know they will drop to the ground, (remember this is because of the pulling force of gravity) but what else might happen?

Hold a balloon as high up as you can and drop it onto the paper—does it break? If not, what do you think you could do to make it splat and why?

Try dropping paint-filled balloons from different heights and observe how the splatter pattern changes. What do you think might be different about a splat from a low height and one from higher up? Why do you think this is?

Don't forget to clear up the balloon pieces afterward as these can be harmful to animals.

✬ MORE FUN

Try dropping an air-filled balloon and a paint/water-filled balloon at the same time. Do you think they will hit the ground simultaneously or at different times? Why do you think this is?

✬ LEARNING POINTS

This activity uses paint-filled water balloons to demonstrate the force of gravity pulling an object down to Earth. The paint gives a great visual of the impact of the balloon hitting the ground, allowing you to compare how the speed of the balloon at impact changes the size of the paint splat. Remember, the greater the height an object falls from, the more speed it has when it hits the ground.

ROCKET BLASTER

This Rocket Blaster is a great fun way to learn about gravity and trajectory. When you pull back and release the mechanism, you should notice that the pom-poms inside don't fall straight to the ground. This is because there are two forces acting on them. Gravity tries to pull the pom-poms down while the forward force from the inner tube propels them forward. These two forces create a curved path to the ground.

- ✿ Rubber band
- ✿ 2 cardboard tubes about 12 inches (30 cm) long (one should fit inside the other)
- ✿ Screwdriver, or something else to make a hole with
- ✿ Cardstock or plastic lid, for the inner cardboard tube
- ✿ Tape
- ✿ Small round pom-poms
- ✿ Paper, for decoration
- ✿ Paint, for decoration

Cut the rubber band so that it forms a single length, then take the wider tube and make a hole using a screwdriver through both sides about 1 inch (3 cm) from one end.

For the smaller tube, make two more holes close to the middle, making sure there is enough of the narrower tube sticking out of the bottom of the larger tube when you put them inside each other for you to hold.

Seal one end of the narrow tube with a piece of cardstock and tape. You can decorate the outside with paper or paint, if desired.

Align the holes by placing the smaller tube inside the larger one (the sealed end of the narrow tube should be inside the wider tube) and thread the rubber band through all the holes. Attach each end of the rubber band to the outside of the wider tube with tape. To test if the mechanism works, pull the inner tube down and let go.

Drop some pom-poms inside the mechanism, pull back the inner tube and let go. The pom-poms should fly through the air.

✿ MORE FUN

What happens if you use bigger pom-poms, do they fly as far?

Can you measure how far different-sized pom-poms travel?

✿ LEARNING POINTS

A real rocket needs to overcome the force of gravity pulling it downward, which it does by creating an upward thrust force from its engines. The thrust force upward must be greater than the downward gravitational force for a rocket to lift off.

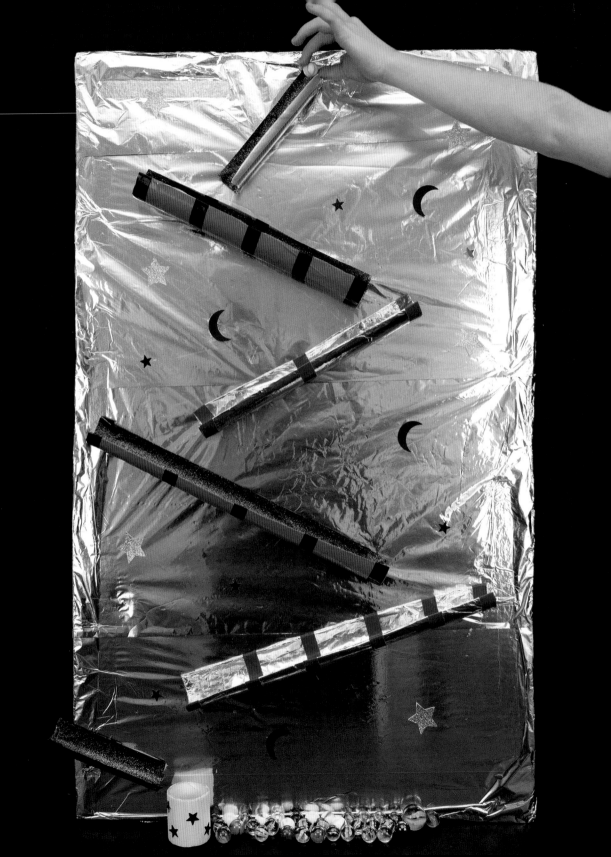

SPACE MARBLE RUN

✿ SCIENTIFIC CONCEPTS—FRICTION, GRAVITY

A great marble run is constructed so the marbles keep rolling all the way to the end, which might be more difficult that it sounds. To keep your marble rolling, you need to understand the forces acting on it.

Gravity pulls down on the marble forcing it to roll down any slopes on the track. While gravity is forcing a marble down a track, frictional forces are slowing the marble down as the marble and marble run rub against each other. The marble will stop if the force of friction is greater than the force of gravity.

- ✿ Long cardboard tubes, cut in half
- ✿ Large sheet of thick cardboard
- ✿ Tape or glue
- ✿ Marbles
- ✿ Aluminum foil, colored cardstock and paint to decorate
- ✿ Bubble wrap, optional
- ✿ Paper towels or kitchen roll, optional

Cut the cardboard tubes into different lengths. These should all be shorter than the width of the large sheet of cardboard. Try placing them down on the large cardboard sheet and start to plan the marble run. Would you like a long, slow marble run, or a quick, fast run? Think about how to position the tubes to make the marble run fast and how you would change them to make it slower. Attach the tubes using tape or glue.

Think about how the marble will roll. It will roll downwards because of gravity and slow down because of friction, but how could you get the marble to roll upwards? You'll need it to be travelling fast enough to overcome gravity. Try a tube with a steep drop followed by a smaller slope upwards. You might have to experiment with different slopes to allow the marble to reach the top of the upward slope.

Use aluminum foil, colored cardstock and paint to decorate your marble run.

Test your marble run using a marble. Does it work as you expected?

✿ MORE FUN

Split into two teams with a group of friends and see who can make the best track to keep a marble rolling for the longest amount of time. Each team should start with the same length of tubing.

Can you change the surface of your tubes so the marble moves more slowly? Try bubble wrap or paper towels on the inside. These surfaces are rougher than the inside of a cardboard tube so the frictional force will be greater, meaning the marble moves more slowly.

✿ LEARNING POINTS

How do you think you could make a very long marble run?

Hint—you'll need to create a very slightly sloping track which is just steep enough to overcome friction and keep the marble rolling.

GRAVITY PINBALL MACHINE

✪ SCIENTIFIC CONCEPT—GRAVITY

If you tried the Space Marble Run (page 19), you'll know that two of the forces acting on a moving object are gravity and friction. A pinball machine is a bit different, as it needs to overcome gravity to shoot a marble or small ball uphill, which can then make its own way down due to gravity.

There are lots of things to think about when making a pinball machine. You need a mechanism to shoot the ball upwards so it falls down quickly; objects down the center to slow the fall of the marble; and if you're feeling very adventurous, you could even make a flipper to flip the marble upwards again.

- ✪ Cardboard box
- ✪ Small cardboard tubes
- ✪ Straws
- ✪ Tape
- ✪ Craft knife
- ✪ Strips of cardboard
- ✪ Marble or small ball

You'll need a shallow box to make a good pinball machine. Make sure you've removed the top so you have a base with fours edges before starting.

You'll need a mechanism to shoot the marble up the ramp. Either use two cardboard tubes, one of which fits inside the other, or a bundle of straws taped together to make the inner tube. You can also make this in a similar way to the Rocket Blaster on page 16.

Once you've made the mechanism and attached it to one side of the pinball machine box, you'll need to make a hole in the box using a craft knife where you want the mechanism to sit. Add a strip of cardboard to the corner of the box above the launch mechanism so the marble curves around the top of the box rather the dropping straight back down.

Think about how to set up obstacles on the inside. If you want the marble to drop down the pinball machine quickly, make the ramps steep. If you want the marble to roll more slowly, make the ramps more gradual.

✪ MORE FUN

Try adding some holes that the marble will drop through if it rolls over them. What else could you add to the pinball machine to slow the descent of the marble or speed it up?

Change the incline of your pinball machine by leaning it on a stack of books. You should find the marble drops down the pinball machine faster with a steeper slope.

✪ LEARNING POINTS

Several factors will affect how fast your marble drops. First is the slope of the pinball machine. A steep slope will mean the ball falls faster. You can slow the fall by adding ramps on the inside. A long gradual ramp will reduce the speed the ball is traveling at more than a short steep ramp, so think about how you'd like the marble to travel before making your plan.

DROP THE ASTRONAUT

✿ SCIENTIFIC CONCEPT—GRAVITY

Have you ever accidentally dropped an egg on the floor and watched it smash? When you drop an object, it is pulled to the ground by gravity, picking up speed as it falls. Remember gravity is a force that pulls an object to the ground.

One way to stop an egg from smashing when it hits the floor is to create an outer casing that reduces the impact of the hard landing on the egg. If you want to make this activity a little less messy, you could boil your astronaut eggs!

✿ Cardboard tubes

✿ Colored cardstock for decoration

✿ Eggs (boiled for less mess)

✿ Cotton wool, bubble wrap, paper towels, pasta

✿ Tape

✿ Tape measure or ruler

Your challenge is to create a safe rocket to allow your eggy astronaut to reach the ground without a single crack.

First, decorate the cardboard tubes so they look like rockets. Think about how you can protect the eggs so they don't break when they hit the ground.

Wrap an egg in cotton wool inside a tube. Remember to make sure there's enough cotton wool to stop the egg from moving. You could also try bubble wrap, paper towels, pasta or anything else you think might protect the egg. When you're ready, seal the bottom with tape.

Once the rockets are prepared, think about the type of surface you want to drop them on. You want a hard surface to really put your protection methods to the test. When you're ready, drop the protected astronaut from as far up as you can reach.

When experimenting, it's important to make the tests fair, so use a ruler or tape measure to make sure you drop each egg rocket from the same height. Or, you could ask the same person to drop them from as far up as they can reach.

✿ MORE FUN

Blow the contents out of an egg so you have just the shell. Draw on the shell so it looks like an astronaut and package it up to send to a friend. Can you package it so well that the eggshell arrives at its destination completely intact?

FLY WITH MAGNETS

☆ SCIENTIFIC CONCEPTS—MAGNETISM, GRAVITY

Rockets overcome the force of gravity trying to pull them back down to earth by generating a massive amount of thrust, which pushes the rocket upwards.

This simple trick shows how to overcome gravity not by generating thrust, but by using a little magnet trickery.

Magnets have two poles: a north pole and south pole. If you place two magnets together end to end, opposite poles will attract and be drawn to each other, while like poles repel each other.

Magnets also attract some metals (like iron and steel), a feature which this activity takes advantage of.

- ☆ Black and white cardstock
- ☆ Cardboard box
- ☆ Chalk
- ☆ Double-sided tape
- ☆ Thin thread
- ☆ Steel paper clip
- ☆ Magnet

Magnets should always be used with adult supervision to avoid swallowing.

Think about the space scene you'd like to create. Would you like the astronaut to be on the Moon, or floating in space? Will they be exploring Mars or traveling farther afield?

Cut out a piece of the black cardstock to fit tightly inside the box and draw a space themed scene on the cardstock using chalk. This will form the background for the magnetic box. Attach the card to the back of the cardboard box using the double-sided tape.

Tie the thin thread to the paper clip and place the magnet on top of the box. Check that the paper clip is attracted to the magnet through the box. If it's not, you'll need a stronger magnet.

Attach the non-paper clip end of the thread to the bottom of the box using tape, remembering to leave just enough length so the paper clip seems to float in the air. Once you've mastered suspending the paper clip, draw a small astronaut or rocket on white card or paper and attach it to the paper clip. You should now have a rocket or astronaut flying in space!

☆ MORE FUN

Try moving the magnet around. Can you make your astronaut or rocket spin or fly around?

What's the biggest gap between the box lid and paper clip you can create without the paper clip falling down?

☆ LEARNING POINTS

The magnetic force between the paper clip and magnet on the top of the box is stronger than gravity's pull. This means the paper clip remains suspended in the air rather than falling to the ground. If you move the paper clip farther from the magnet, the pull of the magnet becomes less. This makes gravity the stronger force acting on the paper clip, which drops to the ground.

FANTASTIC FRICTION

One of the forces acting on a rocket as it flies through the air is the drag between the surface of the rocket and the air. Drag can be thought of as aerodynamic friction. Rockets are streamlined to reduce the effect of drag.

Friction is a force which slows movement between two objects in contact with each other. Imagine two pieces of ribbon rubbing together: the motion feels smooth as there isn't much friction to slow it down. Now imagine rubbing two pieces of kitchen towel together: The motion will be much slower because there is more friction. If you wanted to ski fast down a hill, you'd want your skis to be smooth. Rougher skis would create more friction between them and the snow, slowing you down.

The amount of friction between two objects depends on what the objects are made from, as the rougher the surface, the more friction produced. The more streamlined a rocket is (like being made of metal), the more easily air can flow over the surface, which reduces the slowing effect of friction.

LIFT IT!

☆ SCIENTIFIC CONCEPT—FRICTION

This activity is a great demonstration of friction and a fun trick to show your friends, too! Tell them you can lift a bottle with a pencil without the pencil touching the sides and see if they think you can do it. Remember friction is one of the forces acting on a rocket as it flies through the air.

☆ Funnel

☆ Small plastic water bottle

☆ Rice, uncooked

☆ Pencil

Use the funnel to fill the bottle up with rice, leaving just a bit of space at the top. Tap the bottle's base on a flat surface to let the rice settle.

Carefully push a pencil into the bottle of rice and then pull up again gently. Repeat this motion until the pencil becomes harder and harder to pull out of the bottle as the amount of friction between the pencil and rice increases.

Once the pencil is stuck, try to lift up the bottle of rice with the pencil.

☆ MORE FUN

What happens if you use less rice?

☆ LEARNING POINTS

As you push the pencil into the bottle the grains of rice are being pushed together, rubbing up against each other, creating friction. Eventually the rice grains push against the pencil with enough friction to keep the pencil stuck in place.

FRICTION RAMP

✿ SCIENTIFIC CONCEPT—FRICTION

Have you ever tried sliding on a wooden floor? It's much easier to slide when you wear socks because there is less friction between the smooth surface of the socks and the floor than your feet and the floor. A rocket trying to reach space must overcome the slowing effect of friction.

This Friction Ramp is a great way to demonstrate how the amount of friction changes depending on the material used.

You should find the cars move more slowly down the rougher materials, as there is more friction between them.

✿ Large cardboard sheet

✿ Scissors

✿ Bubble wrap

✿ Corrugated paper

✿ Carpet

✿ Cellophane or plastic wrap

✿ Double-sided tape

✿ Building blocks or books

✿ Toy cars

✿ Timer

Your friction ramp can have as many lanes with as many different surfaces as you want. The only limit is the amount of space you have.

Divide the cardboard sheet into lanes of the same size and then cut the materials you want to test to the correct size so they cover each of the lanes completely. Try bubble wrap, corrugated paper, carpet or cellophane. Once you're happy with the layout, use double-sided tape to attach each material to the ramp.

You'll need the ramp to slope downwards, so lean it up against a tower of blocks or books. Using the cars and the timer, record how long it takes for the same car to travel down each lane of the ramp. You'll need to hold the car at the top of the ramp and let it go without pushing it, or the force you push the car with will impact how long it takes to roll down the ramp.

✿ MORE FUN

Can you add a ramp going upwards to the bottom of your friction ramp and record how far each car travels up the second ramp?

✿ LEARNING POINTS

Remember friction is the resistance of motion when one object rubs against another. The rougher the surface, the more friction is created. Have you ever hurt your knee when sliding on carpet? This is because lots of friction is created between your skin and the carpet.

Friction between tires and the road stop cars from skidding. When the road surface is icy, there is less friction, which makes it more likely cars will skid. In wintery conditions, sand is added to roads to make the road surface rougher, increasing friction and reducing the risk of cars sliding around.

ROCKET ZIP LINE

Friction can be used to slow an object down or speed it up. If we increase the frictional force, the object will move more slowly, and if we reduce friction, it will move faster and more easily.

This activity uses a rocket made from a plastic bottle attached to a zip wire. You can make your rocket move quickly down the zip wire by using a smooth string where there will not be much friction between the straw of the rocket and the string. Or, you can use a rough string where increased frictional forces will slow the descent of your rocket.

✡ Straws

✡ Small plastic bottle

✡ Glue

✡ Rough and smooth string

✡ Timer

✡ Pipe cleaners

Attach a straw to the side of a plastic bottle with glue. When this is dry, thread the string through the straw before setting up your zip line wire.

Find a suitable area to set up the zip line wire. You'll need to attach the string to the ground and something higher up so you have a slope. A tree works well if you're outside.

If you want to decorate your plastic bottle, you can, but this isn't necessary. Hold the bottle at the top of the zip wire and release at the same time as starting the timer. Stop the timer when the bottle reaches the bottom.

You can increase the frictional force further by placing a pipe cleaner inside the straw stuck to the bottle. This should make the bottle slide down the zip wire more slowly.

✡ MORE FUN

Try this activity using different types of string to see if increasing friction slows the descent of the bottle. You could set up several zip wires at once and race the bottles with friends, but remember to keep the length and slope of the zip wire the same to make it a fair comparison.

MARVELOUS LAWS OF MOTION

Newton's First Law

Newton's First Law states that an object at rest will remain at rest. It also states that an object in motion will keep moving with the same speed, and in the same direction, unless another force acts on it. If you're standing still and someone pushes you, you will move, but if no force acts on you, you will stay still.

In the case of a rocket, the engine supplies force in the form of thrust. It is this force that makes a rocket lift off the ground. Without an upward force, a rocket would remain on the ground.

If an object is at rest, it isn't moving in relation to its surroundings. Even when we stand still, we are moving because the Earth is spinning and orbiting around the Sun, but in relation to objects around us, we are motionless.

MILK JUG ROCKET CONE

⭐ SCIENTIFIC CONCEPT—NEWTON'S FIRST LAW

A rocket cone is another simple demonstration of Newton's Laws. The rocket cone is at rest on top of the milk jug, but as soon as a force is applied, which in this case is air being forced out of the jug as you squeeze it, the force of the air against the cone sends it shooting upwards.

⭐ Paper

⭐ Tape

⭐ Felt tip pens, optional

⭐ Empty plastic milk container

Create a cone shape using the paper. This should have a diameter of about 6 inches (15 cm), but can be slightly bigger or smaller. Use the tape to hold the cone in place. If you want to decorate the cone with the felt tip pens so it looks more like a rocket, go ahead, but you don't have to.

Next, examine the empty milk container. Try squeezing it gently and then much harder: You should be able to feel the air leaving the bottle with more force when you squeeze hard than when you squeeze gently. It's the air leaving the bottle that is going to propel the cone rocket up into the air.

When you're ready to launch the rocket, place the cone on top of the milk container and squeeze hard. The paper cone should shoot up into the air! Can you measure how high it flies?

⭐ MORE FUN

Try adding fins to your rocket. Does it fly as high? By adding fins, you've increased the mass of the rocket. According to Newton's Second Law (page 39), the acceleration of an object is affected by the mass, so you should find a rocket cone with more mass doesn't accelerate upwards as fast.

What happens if you make the cone bigger?

⭐ LEARNING POINT

You should find that the harder you push the sides of the bottle together the greater the force of the air leaving the bottle and the higher the rocket cone will go.

SAVE THE ROCKET

✡ SCIENTIFIC CONCEPTS—NEWTON'S FIRST LAW, FRICTION, INERTIA

This simple trick demonstrates Newton's First Law. Your rocket blocks will remain still until another force acts on them. The idea is to remove the cloth under the blocks so quickly and smoothly that no force acts on them and they stay in place.

✡ Small piece of smooth cloth

✡ Wooden blocks

Place the cloth on a table so about half is on the table and half is off. The cloth needs to be big enough so you can easily pull the half hanging off the table. The cloth should be smooth to keep the amount of friction between the cloth and the blocks as low as possible. In the center, create a rocket from the wooden blocks. The block rocket is stable and in a state of inertia until a force moves it. If you wobble the table hard enough, the rocket will topple over as a force has acted on it.

Try slowly moving the cloth around at a constant speed—you should find the rocket tower stays in place, moving with the cloth. But if you change direction or jerk the cloth, the rocket should fall over, as the force acting on it is unbalancing.

The next bit is tricky and might require some practice.

Pull the cloth as fast as possible. If you're fast and smooth enough with the motion, you should find your block rocket stays in place.

✡ MORE FUN

Try making your rocket taller; does it make the trick harder?

What do you think would happen if you used a piece of rough material like a thick towel? Remember you need the amount of friction between the cloth and blocks to be very small and a rough surface means more friction.

✡ LEARNING POINT

If you pull the cloth slowly and jerkily, the blocks will topple as there is too much friction, but if you make the movement fast and smooth they should stay in place.

MARVELOUS LAWS OF MOTION

Newton's Second Law

Newton's Second Law states that force is equal to mass times acceleration. Mass is the amount of "stuff" in an object. The mass of an object is always the same, whereas weight changes depending on the gravitational force. Acceleration is a fancy word for "speeding up." It is a measurement of the change in velocity (speed and motion) of an object. In the case of a rocket, the force propelling the rocket upwards is produced from gas pushed out of the engine. The faster the gas accelerates out of the engine, the greater the thrust produced.

As a rocket burns fuel, its mass decreases, which means the acceleration of the rocket increases, and this is why a rocket goes faster and faster as it moves upwards.

ROCKET RACE

⭐ SCIENTIFIC CONCEPT—NEWTON'S SECOND LAW

When designing rockets, careful thought has to be put into how much the rocket weighs, as the heavier the rocket, the greater the thrust needed to lift it.

This activity requires an empty box. If you add extra mass to the box, it should be harder to push or pull. This is because the force needed to move the box is greater when the mass of the box is increased.

⭐ Cardboard boxes

⭐ Chalk

⭐ Wooden blocks, books or willing volunteer

You'll need a flat area of floor or ground for this activity. It can be done inside or outside, but a wooden floor or smooth outdoor surface works best to start. Make sure the box is strong and sturdy.

Draw a start and finish line with chalk about 10 feet (3 m) apart. Place the box at the start line and carefully push it to the finish line.

Next, fill the box with wooden blocks or books, or if the box is big enough, you could ask a friend to sit inside. Carefully try to push the box from the start to the finish line again. You should find it's much harder to push the box when it's heavier.

Is it easier to pull or push?

⭐ MORE FUN

Can you design a handle for the box? Does this make pushing or pulling the box easier?

BALL COLLISION RAMP

☆ SCIENTIFIC CONCEPTS—NEWTON'S SECOND LAW, MOMENTUM

In this activity, you roll a marble down a ramp so it collides with another marble at the bottom. You should find that momentum is conserved during the collision, which means the motion from the marble rolling is transferred to the stationary marble at the bottom of the ramp.

Only moving objects have momentum, but momentum doesn't always stay the same: It changes if the object changes direction, speeds up or slows down.

☆ Thick cardboard

☆ Box or blocks

☆ Marbles or other small balls

☆ Ruler

Create a ramp by placing a sheet of thick cardboard on top of a box or stack of blocks. Place one marble or small ball at the bottom of the ramp and one at the top.

If you let the first marble roll down the ramp, its momentum will increase as it picks up speed. The marble at the bottom of the ramp is stationary until the moving marble hits it. When the two marbles collide, momentum is transferred from the rolling marble to the stationary marble, which then starts to move.

Using the ruler, can you measure how far the stationary marble rolls?

Remember, the total momentum doesn't change. It is conserved.

☆ MORE FUN

Try replacing the marble at the top with a smaller ball. A smaller ball has a smaller mass, therefore a smaller momentum, so you should find the stationary marble doesn't move as far.

☆ LEARNING POINT

You could also think of momentum as how hard it is to stop something from moving. We know it's harder to stop something moving fast than something moving more slowly as the fast moving object has more momentum.

MOON BUGGY RACE

✿ SCIENTIFIC CONCEPT—NEWTON'S SECOND LAW

For a rocket to lift off from its launch pad, the thrust from the engine must be greater than the weight of the rocket. The heavier the rocket, the greater the force needed to move it.

We can demonstrate this very simply using moon buggies. If we make the moon buggies heavier, the force needed to move them is greater.

✿ Large sheet of cardboard

✿ Felt tip pens

✿ Ruler

✿ Small cardboard box

✿ Axles and wheels

✿ Marbles

✿ Pen and paper, to record the results

Draw a road on the large sheet of cardboard using felt tip pens and use a ruler to help you add a scale to the side so you can record how far the moon buggy travels. You then need to draw a start line at the beginning of the scale.

To create a simple moon buggy, carefully make holes in the center of each wheel. These could be lids or circles cut from thick cardboard. Attach a wheel to one end of each axle. Make holes at each end of the cardboard box (this is the body of the moon buggy) for the axles to pass through. Push the axles through the holes and attach the second wheel to each side.

Place one moon buggy at the start line and gently push it. Use the scale to record how far the moon buggy travels. Do this three times and find the average distance moved by adding up each distance and dividing by three (or however many results you have).

After your first test, make the moon buggy heavier. Fill it with marbles and push it using the same force you used for the buggy with no extra load. Do this three times and find the average distance traveled in the same way.

✿ MORE FUN

Investigate what happens if you add even more weight to the moon buggy. Can you predict how far a moon buggy twice as heavy as the first will travel?

Can you think of another way to propel the moon buggy? Could you try blowing it as hard as you can?

✿ LEARNING POINTS

You should find that the heavier moon buggy doesn't move as far; this is because Newton's Second Law states that force equals mass times acceleration, so if you increase the mass, but use the same force the acceleration will be less.

MARVELOUS LAWS OF MOTION

Newton's Third Law

Newton's Third Law states that for every action there is always an equal and opposite reaction. A rocket burns fuel, which forces gas out of its engine. This is the action. The reaction is the creation of thrust, which forces the rocket upwards.

FILM CANISTER ROCKET

⭐ SCIENTIFIC CONCEPT—NEWTON'S LAWS OF MOTION

A film canister rocket is a great demonstration of all three of Newton's Laws of Motion.

Newton's First Law

Newton's First Law states that an object will stay still unless a force acts on it. The film canister remains motionless until we add materials to create a force.

Newton's Second Law

Newton's Second Law states that the acceleration of an object is affected by the mass of an object.

If you make the film canister heavier, you should find it accelerates more slowly than a lighter canister and doesn't fly as high.

Newton's Third Law

Newton's Third Law states that for every action there is an equal and opposite reaction. In the case of the film canister, the downward force of the gas on the canister lid creates an opposite upwards force on the body of the canister which shoots up into the air.

To reach space, a rocket must escape past the Earth's gravitational force, which wants to pull it down. Rockets do this by generating a massive amount of thrust. The engine needs to create the greatest thrust possible in the shortest time in order to overcome gravity. Thrust is created using Newton's Third Law. The combustion of rocket fuel creates hot exhaust gas, which escapes from the rocket producing a downward force, and the reaction force then creates an upward thrust force.

⭐ Goggles

⭐ Chalk

⭐ Film canister

⭐ Water

⭐ Effervescent heartburn or vitamin tablets

⭐ Baking soda

⭐ Tissue

⭐ Vinegar

Find a safe spot to launch the rocket. The launch area needs to be a flat, hard surface, with a safe distance from other people. Use chalk to draw safety lines at least 9 feet (3 m) from the rocket. Observers should stay behind the lines.

(continued)

FILM CANISTER ROCKET (CONTINUED)

Decide which rocket fuel (effervescent vitamin/heartburn tablets or baking soda and vinegar) you want to test first and think how you're going to decide which is the best fuel. Will it be the one that makes the rocket fly the highest and fastest? Or the one that uses the least fuel, makes the least mess and is the easiest to use?

Remember that the film canister rockets fly upwards very quickly, so be sure to wear safety goggles and stand back.

Effervescent Heartburn or Vitamin Tablets

Fill the film canister halfway with water and place one tablet inside. Carefully replace the lid and put the canister in the launch area with the lid on the floor. Remember the film canisters fly upwards very quickly, so stand back immediately and ask an adult to help.

Baking Soda and Vinegar

Wrap a couple of teaspoons of baking soda inside a tissue, and then fill the film canister halfway with vinegar. Drop the tissue-wrapped baking soda inside and replace the lid. Put the canister lid down in the launch area and stand back. Ask an adult to help.

⭐ MORE FUN

Can you decorate your film canister to look more like a rocket? Do you think the extra weight will affect how the rocket flies?

⭐ LEARNING POINTS

When water is added to the heartburn or vitamin tablets, they start to break down, releasing carbon dioxide gas. The buildup of carbon dioxide inside the canister creates pressure, which builds up until eventually it becomes strong enough to force the cap down, which in turn forces the canister part upwards. Newton's Third Law is at work again.

The baking soda and vinegar rocket needs to have the baking soda wrapped in tissue to stop the baking soda from reacting with the vinegar too quickly. If most of the gas is released before you can replace the lid, the pressure inside the canister won't be enough for it to launch.

STREAMLINE A BOTTLE ROCKET

⭐ SCIENTIFIC CONCEPTS—DRAG, AIR RESISTANCE

Drag, or air resistance, doesn't affect rockets once they have reached space as there is no air there, but it does affect a rocket trying to get to space. There are four forces that act on a rocket. These are lift, drag, weight and thrust. Drag is similar to friction and is affected by the size and shape of the rocket. Some shapes create less drag as air passes over them more easily. Imagine a ball falling to the ground, pushing air particles out of the way as it falls.

The more streamlined an object is, the more easily air can flow over the surface, causing less air resistance.

Challenge—reduce drag so your rocket flies for longer!

- ⭐ Water Powered Bottle Rocket (page 52)
- ⭐ Cardstock
- ⭐ Tape
- ⭐ Foot pump with needle adapter
- ⭐ Cork that fits the bottle opening
- ⭐ Water
- ⭐ Goggles
- ⭐ Timer

The nose cone of a rocket is the pointy bit at the end. This is the first part of the rocket to meet the air and its shape and size affect the amount of air resistance created as a rocket flies through the air. You can test different nose cone shapes to investigate how each affects how the rocket flies.

Think about what shapes of nose cone you'd like to test. You could try a cone, hemisphere, pyramid or a flat end. Can you think of any other shapes that would work?

Set up the bottle rocket with the foot pump, cork and water as on page 52.

Construct various nose cones from cardstock in different shapes and sizes. Add each test cone one by one, using tape to attach them.

Always wear safety goggles when launching bottle rockets.

Launch each rocket and record how long it stays in the air using the timer. Remember everything must be the same apart from the cone for each launch.

⭐ MORE FUN

What else could you change to make the rocket more or less streamlined?

⭐ LEARNING POINTS

The shape of a rocket's nose cone, its diameter and the speed it's traveling all affect the amount of air resistance slowing it down. Narrow rockets (small diameter) and an aerodynamic nose cone both help to reduce the amount of air resistance created.

A more streamlined nose cone should mean that the bottle rocket flies for longer as there is less air resistance to slow it down.

WATER-POWERED BOTTLE ROCKET

☆ SCIENTIFIC CONCEPT—NEWTON'S LAWS OF MOTION

A bottle rocket is another great demonstration of all of Newton's Three Laws of Motion. The rocket remains motionless unless a force acts on it (Newton's First Law). The amount of force is affected by the amount of air pumped into the rocket and the force can be increased by adding water (Newton's Second Law). Air and water being forced from the nozzle creates an equal and opposite reaction force which propels the rocket upwards (Newton's Third Law).

Pressure builds up inside the bottle when air is pumped into it. When the pressure is enough to force out the cork, water shoots from bottle downwards, making the bottle push back upward, forcing it into the air.

- ☆ Empty plastic bottle
- ☆ Paint, optional
- ☆ Duct tape, optional
- ☆ Cardstock and transparent tape, optional
- ☆ Foot pump with a needle adaptor
- ☆ Cork that fits the bottle opening
- ☆ Water
- ☆ Goggles

Please make sure an adult is around as the rocket takes off very suddenly and forcefully. Do not approach the rocket once you have started pumping!

If you want to decorate the bottle to look more like a space rocket, you can paint it, cover it with duct tape and/or use cardstock attached with tape to make a nose cone and fins. Just remember adding extra weight will affect how the bottle rocket flies. If you do add fins, try to make them strong enough so the rocket can stand up on them. If the fins aren't strong enough, you'll need to build something to hold the rocket upright.

Push the needle adaptor of the pump through the cork: it needs to go all the way through to allow air into the bottle.

Add water to the bottle so it's about one quarter full. Once you've added water, push the cork in. This should be a very tight fit so no air can escape.

Always wear safety goggles when launching a bottle rocket.

When you're happy with the rocket, take it outside and connect the pump to the needle adaptor. Ask an adult to slowly pump air into the bottle. Remember to ask any spectators to stand well back as the rocket will fly upwards quickly.

☆ MORE FUN

Try adding extra weight to your rocket. What do you think will happen?

☆ LEARNING POINT

Instead of using water, a real rocket burns fuel to create a hot gas. The hot gas escaping downward from the rocket pushes the rocket upward and it is this creation of thrust that allows a rocket to overcome gravity and blast off into space.

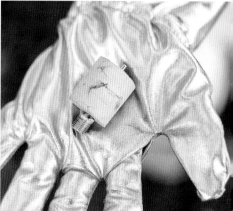

AMAZING AIR RESISTANCE

Air resistance (also known as drag) is one of the forces acting on a rocket as it takes off.

When a rocket first takes off, gravity pulls it back down to Earth while the thrust force created by the rocket engines pushes it upwards.

As the rocket gains in speed, air resistance increases, slowing down the rocket. For a rocket to fly upward, the thrust force must be greater than air resistance slowing it down and the effect of gravity to pull the rocket back to Earth.

The faster a rocket travels, the more air it has to push out of the way and the more air resistance it experiences. Air resistance can be reduced by streamlining rockets to make air pass over them more smoothly.

COFFEE FILTER PARACHUTE

⭐ SCIENTIFIC CONCEPTS—AIR RESISTANCE, DRAG, SURFACE AREA

When rockets return to Earth, parachutes can be used to slow their descent. These parachutes are a fun way to learn about air resistance. We know that air resistance slows the fall of an object and it increases with surface area. This means a bigger parachute should slow the fall of an object the most.

Can you test this?

⭐ Coffee filters, different sizes

⭐ Hole punch

⭐ String

⭐ Small containers

⭐ Small toy figure or paper clips

Make four small holes evenly spaced around the edges of each coffee filter using a hole punch. These will act as the parachute sheets.

Cut out enough pieces of string for all the parachutes you want to make. You'll need four for each parachute and they should all be the same length, it doesn't matter too much how long the string is, but about as long as your arm will work well.

Carefully tie a piece of string to each parachute hole, and attach the other ends evenly around a small container.

Try adding small objects such as small toy figure, paper clips or anything that will add weight to the parachute to the small container.

Drop each parachute and time how long they take to reach the ground.

Remember that to test each parachute fairly, you need to use the same objects in the container and drop each from the same height.

⭐ MORE FUN

What do you think will happen if you add more weight to the parachute?

⭐ LEARNING POINT

You should find that a bigger parachute catches the air better than a small parachute to slow the fall. This is because a bigger parachute has a larger surface area and creates more air resistance, slowing the fall.

FEEL THE FORCE

Rockets are made smooth and pointy to reduce the amount of air resistance acting on them when they take off. Reducing air resistance in this way is called making something streamlined.

⚡ Large sheet of paper or cardstock

⚡ Stick

⚡ Tape

⚡ Empty water bottle

⚡ Scissors

Attach a large piece of cardstock to the end of the stick. Make sure you have lots of space and wave the stick around. Put an empty water bottle on the floor and try to blow it over by moving the air close to the bottle with your stick.

Use the scissors to make the cardstock stuck to the stick smaller by about ¾ inch (2 cm) from each edge. Wave the stick around and try to blow the bottle over again. Keep reducing the size of the cardstock by ¾ inch (2 cm) and note down how if feels when you wave it and how easy it is to blow the bottle over.

You should find that it feels harder to move the stick when the cardstock is bigger as there is more air resistance acting on it. The bottle should be easier to knock over the bigger the cardstock is as more air is being pushed out of the way.

⚡ MORE FUN

Try the investigation again using different sizes of cardstock.

Drop a folded piece of cardstock and an open piece of cardstock of the same size to the ground from the same height. What happens?

⚡ LEARNING POINTS

If you run faster, you should find that you feel even more air resistance. This is because when you run faster you push more air out of the way, which then pushes back more.

LET'S GLIDE

Everything flying through the air has four forces acting on it: thrust, drag, lift and gravity. Rockets are straight and thin to reduce drag, helping them reach the incredible speeds needed to escape the Earth's gravitational force.

This glider is the opposite of a rocket in that it has big wings to increase drag, so it can stay in the air longer.

☆ Straws or pipe cleaners

☆ Tissue paper, paper, contact paper or cardstock

☆ Tape

Think about what shape you'd like the glider to be. You could try a square, triangle, cube or hexagon: the choice is yours.

Create the shape using straws or pipe cleaners and cover with your choice of paper. A good glider to practice with is a triangle covered in tissue paper. The tissue paper is light and the triangle shape makes it strong.

Try throwing the glider from a height and measure how far it flies. Investigate using lots of different shapes and materials to find the best combination.

☆ MORE FUN

Can you time how long the glider flies in the air?

☆ LEARNING POINT

A glider with a bigger surface area should fly for longer as it creates more air resistance, which slows its fall.

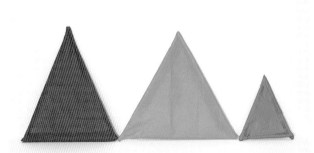

LET'S LAUNCH!

If you blow up a balloon and let it go, the air rushes out of the balloon in one direction while the balloon moves in the opposite direction, making it fly around the room. This effect is used to propel a rocket into space.

When a rocket launches, hot exhaust gases are created and released through the engine nozzle at high speed. This downward force creates an upward thrust force (Newton's Third Law) pushing the rocket upward.

A tiny balloon flies around the room easily, but imagine how heavy a rocket is and how much force is needed for it to leave the ground! Rockets burn a huge amount of fuel to overcome the forces of air resistance and gravity trying to slow and pull them down.

Rockets are usually made up of several stages—when one has used its fuel, it's discarded to reduce the weight of the rocket and save fuel. Discarded stages usually either burn up in the atmosphere or fall back to Earth.

MOBILE LAUNCH PAD

Mobile launch platforms were used to transport the Saturn V rockets and space shuttles to the launch pad. A mobile launch pad has to be able to hold a huge amount of weight and be capable of moving.

For this activity, you're going to think about how to construct a strong, stable structure by considering what makes a strong shape.

A triangle is stronger than a square as it has only three points of connection and any load applied is equally spread through the shape. Engineers often add a diagonal section to a square (making it into two triangles and therefore stronger).

☆ Pen and paper

☆ Medium piece of cardboard

☆ Scissors

☆ 2 axles

☆ 2 straws

☆ Wheels

☆ Tape

☆ Small piece of cardboard

☆ Wooden blocks

Think about the properties your mobile launch pad should have. It needs to be light enough to move, yet strong enough to hold something heavy. Draw a design for your launch pad using pen and paper, thinking about strong shapes.

The medium piece of cardboard will be the base of the vehicle. Cut the axles so they are $1/3$ inch (1 cm) longer than the width of the base, then cut 2 straws so they are about $1/2$ inch (1.5 cm) shorter than the axles and thread each axle through a straw. Attach the wheels to the end of each axle. The straw should be able to move freely around the axle. Jar lids or CDs make good wheels.

Attach the axles and wheels to the underside of the base with tape. Check that the wheels turn easily.

Once you have a base, create a platform using straws and a small piece of cardboard. Remember to think about the shapes you use, as triangles are stronger than squares.

Test your platform by adding something heavy like wooden blocks to the top. Remember, rockets are very, very heavy!

*See photo on page 60.

☆ MORE FUN

Try to build a bridge using half eggshells. The shell itself is very brittle, but the dome shape makes it strong.

☆ LEARNING POINTS

A dome is very good at spreading weight evenly in all directions so that no part of the dome has to support more weight than another part. If you have four half eggshells, you can balance a stack of books on top of them without causing damage because of the dome shape.

ROCKET LAUNCH STATION FOR A BOTTLE ROCKET

⭐ SCIENTIFIC CONCEPT—GRAVITY

The challenge with this investigation is to build a stand to hold a bottle rocket. The stand should allow the rocket to stand upright before launch, but not restrict it from taking off.

⭐ Bottle Rocket and foot pump (page 52)

⭐ Straws

⭐ Cardboard box

⭐ Scissors

⭐ Cardboard tubes

⭐ Tape

⭐ Goggles

First make a bottle rocket. See page 52 for instructions.

Construct the stand, remembering it must support the weight of your bottle rocket and remain on the ground when the rocket takes off.

You can use any materials you want for this activity: It can be as simple or complex as you like. You could start with a very simple design using 4 straws taped to the side of the bottle rocket to help it stand up. Make a stand with the cardboard box by cutting a hole in the top using scissors so the bottle rocket sits with just the bottleneck in the hole. Cut a hole in the side of the box to allow the tubing from the foot pump to fit through.

To use cardboard tubes, make these into a square shape and attach together with tape, the square should be just big enough so the bottom of the rocket sits nicely inside with the rest of the bottle rocket on top.

For an extra challenge, you could build clamps to hold the rocket in place until it's time for take off.

Be careful to leave space for the pump to attach to the cork in the rocket.

Once you're happy with your design, can you test it? Remember a bottle rocket should be vertical at liftoff.

Always wear safety goggles and ask an adult to help.

⭐ MORE FUN

Can you build a launch station using just one material? Or how about a launch station that will stay upright on a windy day?

CRAZY COMBUSTION AND CHEMICAL REACTIONS

For a rocket to escape from the Earth's gravity and enter orbit around the planet, it needs to travel very quickly, which requires a massive amount of energy. To reach such high speeds, a rocket needs a lot of propellant. Propellant consists of fuel and an oxidizer (a chemical that releases oxygen and is needed to make the fuel burn).

Gases forced out of the engine at high speed propel the rocket upwards. The huge amount of fuel needed to overcome the Earth's gravity adds a lot of weight to the rocket, which is why most are made up of two or three stages. Once each stage has used its fuel, it separates from the main body of the rocket to reduce the weight.

Rockets use fuel and an oxidizer, which react inside a combustion chamber. This reaction produces hot gases. We can't copy this reaction at home as it would be very dangerous, but we can create simple (and safe) chemical reactions using baking soda and vinegar, which also release a gas.

BALLOON ROCKET

✡ SCIENTIFIC CONCEPT—CHEMICAL REACTIONS

Vinegar is an acid and baking soda is a base. When an acid and a base are mixed together, they react to neutralize each other, releasing carbon dioxide gas. This is an example of a chemical reaction. The baking soda and vinegar have to come into contact with each other to react, like the fuel and oxidizer in a rocket.

The carbon dioxide fills the bottle and then the balloon. If enough gas enters the balloon, the balloon will blow up.

✡ Balloon

✡ Felt tip pens

✡ 2 tsp (9 g) baking soda

✡ Small bottle

✡ 10 tsp (50 ml) vinegar

Blow up the balloon a little and let the air out. This allows the balloon to expand more easily when the gas from the chemical reaction enters it.

Draw a rocket on the balloon using a felt tip pen. This is easiest to do when the balloon is blown up, but don't tie it off.

Place the baking soda into the bottle followed by the vinegar, and then quickly place the balloon over the bottle opening. You should be able to see the baking soda and vinegar react as lots of bubbles appear. The bubbles are carbon dioxide, which is released in the neutralization reaction between the baking soda and vinegar.

The carbon dioxide produced in the reaction will first fill the bottle and then the balloon making it increase in size.

✡ MORE FUN

Experiment using different amounts of baking soda and vinegar. Which combination gives you the biggest balloon?

SPEED IT UP

✡ SCIENTIFIC CONCEPT—CHEMICAL REACTIONS

Reactants are substances you combine to get a reaction. Some react slowly and some much faster, depending on the bonds that need to be broken. For example, gold is very nonreactive, while sodium and potassium are so reactive that they tarnish instantly when exposed to the air. Rocket scientists need to be able to control the speed of the combustion reactions. This is usually done by controlling the speed at which fuel is pumped into the combustion chamber.

Increasing the concentration of reactants and the temperature at which the reaction takes place can speed up chemical reactions.

- ✡ 2 balloons
- ✡ Felt tip pens
- ✡ Warm and cold water
- ✡ Small bottles
- ✡ Effervescent heartburn or vitamin tablets

Blow up the balloons a little and let the air out. Draw a rocket on each balloon using a felt tip pen. Remember not to seal the balloon end.

Carefully pour the warm water into one bottle and the cold into another bottle so each is about one third full. The same amount of water should be used in each so this is a fair test.

Place one tablet into each bottle then quickly place the balloons over the bottle openings. If you watch carefully, you should see that the tablet in the warm water reacts faster than the tablet in cold water and is used up first. The balloon on the warm water bottle should blow up first as carbon dioxide is released faster in that reaction.

✡ MORE FUN

Try the investigation again but this time use two tablets and cold water. What do you think will happen?

✡ LEARNING POINTS

The higher the concentration, the faster the reaction, this is because there is more of the reactive substance available to react.

The higher the temperature, the faster the reaction: heating up a substance causes the particles to have more energy and move around faster, meaning they have more contact with the other reactive substance.

WHICH NOZZLE SIZE?

✡ SCIENTIFIC CONCEPTS—THRUST, LIFT, CHEMICAL REACTIONS

Earlier activities have shown that thrust to lift the rocket is created when the fuel burns. The nozzle is the part of a rocket through which the hot gases from the burning of the fuel escape. This reduces the opening through which gases can escape and so increases the acceleration of the gases as they leave the rocket, maximizing thrust.

✡ Garden hose with a spray attachment

✡ Chalk, optional

✡ Syringes with different width openings

✡ Paint, optional

✡ White sheet, optional

To test how a nozzle works, set up a garden hose with a spray attachment and turn it on. First try opening the nozzle as wide as it will go and measure how far the water squirts out. If you do this outside on a dry patio, you could use chalk to mark the farthest distance the spray reaches.

Set the nozzle as small as it will go and mark how far the water squirts. You should find that a smaller hole for the water to be squirted from means it leaves the hose with more force and travels farther. Can you feel the extra thrust when the nozzle opening is smaller?

✡ MORE FUN

Try squirting water through syringes with different size openings. You should find water travels farther the smaller the opening, and it should feel harder to push the water out of a small syringe. Why do you think this is?

If you're feeling creative, try filling the syringes with paint, then squirt them onto an old white sheet. Are narrower or wider syringes better for reaching the sheet if you take a few steps backward?

BAKING SODA-POWERED CORK ROCKET

⭐ SCIENTIFIC CONCEPT—CHEMICAL REACTIONS

Baking soda and vinegar react to neutralize each other, releasing carbon dioxide. We can use this reaction to make a mini cork rocket.

⭐ Goggles

⭐ Cork

⭐ Small plastic carbonated beverage bottle

⭐ 1 tbsp (13 g) baking soda

⭐ Paper towels or kitchen roll

⭐ ⅓ cup (70 ml) vinegar

This must be done outside as the cork will shoot up into the air very quickly and with force. Remember to wear eye protection.

Make sure the cork fits inside the top of the empty bottle. It should be a snug fit because you don't want any of the gas to escape. When you're happy with the fit, remove the cork and set it aside.

If you put the baking soda in the bottle on its own, when you add the vinegar, the reaction will happen so fast that most of the gas released by the reaction will be lost in the time it takes to get the cork on. To solve this problem, wrap the baking soda in a paper towel and push it into the bottle. Add the vinegar and push the cork in tightly while keeping the bottle facing away from you in case the cork flies off quickly.

Once the cork is in place, put the bottle down and stand back as soon as you can. The cork will fly through the air with a bang when the pressure inside is strong enough.

⭐ MORE FUN

Try adding a cone and ribbons to your cork. Do these affect how it flies?

PUMP IT OUT

✬ SCIENTIFIC CONCEPT—CHEMICAL REACTIONS

Rocket engines use pumps to mix their fuel and oxidizer in a combustion chamber. The amount of fuel and oxidizer pumped into the combustion chambers controls the amount of thrust generated.

This activity uses very simple pumps found in hand soap containers to mix paint, which is much less explosive but lots of fun.

✬ 2 empty hand soap containers with a pump

✬ Water and paint or food coloring

✬ Large, flat container

✬ Baking soda

✬ Vinegar

✬ Dish soap

The empty soap dispensers are the pumps and the container is the combustion chamber. We can't burn fuel but we can try some color mixing!

Half fill your hand soap containers with different color paints and pump out some paint from each into the large container. You could have black paint in one pump and white in another, and then vary the amount of white paint you pump compared to black to get different shades of grey. Or you could mix blue and yellow to make green, red and yellow to make orange, or red and blue to make purple.

Can you pump both colors into the container at the same time?

✬ MORE FUN

Mix a couple of tablespoons of baking soda with water to put in one dispenser and fill the other with vinegar. If you pump both into your container, you should see a neutralization reaction take place with bubbles of gas given off. Try adding dish soap and food coloring to get a lovely thick colorful foam.

✬ LEARNING POINT

The baking soda and vinegar react only when they are mixed. In a rocket engine combustion occurs only when the fuel and oxidizer are released into the combustion chamber.

TRICKY TRAJECTORY

Trajectory is the path an object follows as it flies through the air. Imagine the path a ball takes when you throw it. If you throw the ball straight upward, its trajectory is different than if you throw it forward toward someone else.

Rockets initially fly vertically upward through the lower, denser parts of the atmosphere but then turn so they are on the correct path to enter orbit around the Earth.

This means their overall trajectory is a curved path, rather than the vertical path you might expect.

SQUEEZY BOTTLE ROCKET

✿ SCIENTIFIC CONCEPT—TRAJECTORY

This easy-to-construct rocket is great for investigating how the angle a rocket is launched from affects its flight. The rockets work because as you squeeze the bottle, air is forced out of the straw in the bottle and pushes against the rocket straw. This force causes the rocket straw to fly through the air.

- ✿ Empty water bottles with a sports cap
- ✿ Scissors
- ✿ 2 straws, 1 wide enough fit over the other
- ✿ Modeling clay
- ✿ Cardstock or paper
- ✿ Felt tip pens
- ✿ Tape

To make the bottle part of the rocket, it's really important to make sure the sports cap is completely airtight. If air can escape, your rocket won't fly very far.

Cut the thinner straw into quarters and put one segment into the center of the sports cap. Seal the straw around the cap using modeling clay. You can check the seal is complete by squeezing the bottle: If the seal is secure, all of the air from the bottle should come out of the straw, not the bottle neck. This is your rocket launcher!

To make the rocket part, first cut the wider straw into quarters and seal one end with tape; this is to stop air from escaping. Draw a rocket shape with felt tip pens on the cardstock or paper. Remember, the lighter the rocket, the farther it will fly.

Attach the paper rocket onto one side of the rocket straw using tape and place it onto the straw in the rocket launcher.

Squeeze the rocket launcher hard, and you should find that the rocket shoots up into the air. Try launching at different angles to see how you can make the rocket fly farther.

✿ MORE FUN

Try adding extra weight to your straw rocket by placing a small ball of modeling clay on the end. Does this change how far and for how long it flies?

✿ LEARNING POINTS

You should find that your straw rocket flies farther if you launch at an angle forwards rather than straight up. This is because gravity and the forward force created by the rocket launcher act together to create a curved flight path.

FLIGHT PATH ANGLES

⭐ SCIENTIFIC CONCEPT—ANGLES

If you tried the Squeezy Bottle Rocket (page 76) or Foam Rocket (page 79), you should have found that changing the angle at which you released the rocket altered its flight path.

Angles are very important when navigating spacecraft. For example, for a successful reentry into the Earth's atmosphere, the entry angle has to be within set limits or the spacecraft can break up or bounce back into space.

A protractor is an instrument used to measure angles. This giant version makes it easy to visualize angles and set your rockets to launch at an angle.

⭐ Large sheet of cardboard

⭐ Scissors

⭐ Felt tip pens

⭐ Plates or hula hoop

⭐ Ruler

⭐ Protractor

⭐ Squeezy Bottle Rocket (page 76) or Foam Rocket (page 79)

To make this giant protractor, you need to cut out a big semicircle from the card. You could do this by drawing around half of a plate or hula hoop.

Once you're happy with your semicircle, start by measuring and drawing a 90-degree line with the ruler, drawn up from the center of the card. Then mark 0 and 180 on the bottom line at each end. Carefully fill in the other angles using the small protractor as a guide.

Use the giant protractor to test the rockets at different angles. What do you think will happen if you shoot the rockets straight up?

⭐ MORE FUN

Try using the protractor to release the rockets at different angles and record how far they travel on the ground using chalk.

⭐ LEARNING POINT

Protractors are usually small and made from plastic. This super size protractor makes it easy to check and measure the angle you want to launch your rockets from.

FOAM ROCKET

☆ SCIENTIFIC CONCEPT—TRAJECTORY

Foam rockets work the same way as the Squeezy Bottle Rocket (page 76); you're just using a different material to make the rocket part. If you don't want to make a launcher this time, you can try using just a straw as a launcher and blowing into the straw.

☆ Thin foam pipe insulation

☆ Duct tape

☆ Cardstock for decoration, optional

☆ Tape

☆ Straw

☆ Squeezy Bottle Rocket Launcher (page 76)

Cut a small piece of the foam pipe insulation and seal the end with duct tape. This is your foam rocket. You can make a nose cone and fins using colored cardstock and attach them to the foam rocket with tape if you want.

You can launch your foam rocket with a straw if you don't want to use a bottle launcher like on page 76. First check that the foam rocket fits on top of the straw. If the fit is too tight, either use a thinner straw or try to widen the foam tube by pushing the straw in and out a few times.

When you're happy with the fit, choose a launch angle and blow hard into the straw or use a squeezy bottle rocket launcher. You should find your foam rocket shoots through the air.

☆ MORE FUN

Launch your foam rocket at different angles to investigate which angle allows the rocket to cover the most ground distance.

LIVING IN SPACE

The human body is adapted to live on Earth. We're used to being grounded thanks to gravity, pleasant temperatures, lots of contact with other humans and readily available food. Unlike Earth, space is a highly dangerous, hostile environment. Spacecraft must provide everything an astronaut needs to survive: light, heat, food, water, air to breathe and protection from the hazards of space.

Astronauts experience space sickness, weightlessness, are exposed to high radiation levels and experience loss of bone mass, and that's just inside the spacecraft!

STRONG SUIT

☆ SCIENTIFIC CONCEPT—PROPERTIES OF MATERIALS

A space suit is a vital piece of equipment for astronauts and must protect them from the hazards of space. The suit needs to protect an astronaut from extreme cold, radiation, sunlight and fast moving dust and rocks while providing oxygen, removing carbon dioxide and giving clear vision. It basically has to be a complete life-support system for the wearer.

The materials used to make space suits must be carefully chosen to provide astronauts with all the protection they need from the extreme conditions of space.

In this activity, you're going to freeze different materials to investigate how their properties change when exposed to the cold.

☆ Cotton wool

☆ Felt

☆ Cotton

☆ Bubble wrap

☆ Aluminum foil

☆ Muffin tray, optional

Cut out a small segment of each material you want to test. These should all be roughly the same size. Make a note of how each material feels and how flexible it is.

The muffin tray isn't essential, but will keep each sample separate and stop them from sticking to each other. You need to carefully put a different material in each segment of the tray making sure they aren't touching and place in the freezer for about 2 hours.

Check each material one by one. How have they changed since being in the freezer? Create a table and record your observations before and after freezing. Did any of the materials surprise you? Can you think of anything else to test?

While it's chilly inside your freezer (about 0°F [-17°C]), outer space is much colder, about -455°F (-270°c)!

☆ MORE FUN

Can you design a helmet for an astronaut? Think about what would be useful. How about a camera, light or emergency food supply?

KEEPING WARM

Spacecraft must be able to keep astronauts at a safe and comfortable temperature, protecting them from the extreme temperatures of space. Spacecraft are constructed of special materials to protect astronauts not only from heat and cold, but also radiation.

This activity explores the effect of heat and light from the Sun on objects on Earth.

✧ Ice cubes (should be the same shape and size)

✧ Aluminum foil

✧ Black paper

✧ White paper

✧ Paper towels or kitchen roll

✧ Bubble wrap

✧ Timer or stopwatch

Carefully make ice cubes using the same amount of water for each. The aim of this activity is to slow down the rate at which the ice cubes melt.

Wrap each ice cube in a different material, and leave one unwrapped. The unwrapped ice cube is your control: it means you can see what would happen to the other cubes if they were not wrapped up.

Leave all of the ice cubes in a sunny spot and use a stopwatch to check every 5 minutes to see how much they have melted. Is it easy to tell which have melted the most? If you can't tell easily, you could weigh each cube after 15 minutes.

Which material do you think will protect the cube from melting most efficiently?

✧ MORE FUN

Instead of covering the ice cubes with a material, try leaving them in different places. Good places to leave them are in the Sun, in the shade, in the fridge and on a windowsill. Which do you think will melt first?

SOLAR POWER

The best and most available source of energy for spacecraft is energy from the Sun. Solar rays can be used to convert solar energy to electricity, which can then be used for power. We can harness the energy of the Sun on Earth to make a solar oven.

A solar oven isn't just the Sun heating up the food inside: it's specially designed to utilize the Sun's thermal energy efficiently. Aluminum foil reflects heat and light. This is used to line the lid of the solar oven, which should be positioned to reflect heat onto the food inside the box.

The bottom of the solar oven should be lined with black paper. Black paper absorbs the heat and light reflected onto it by the foil. Plastic food wrap is placed over the top of the oven to stop the warm air heated by the Sun from escaping.

- ⭐ Cardboard box (like a pizza box)
- ⭐ Aluminum foil
- ⭐ Matte black cardstock or paper
- ⭐ Tape
- ⭐ Marshmallows, chocolate, cheese or ice cube
- ⭐ Plate
- ⭐ Plastic wrap
- ⭐ Stick

To prepare the oven, you need to cover the inside lid of the cardboard box with aluminum foil and place matte black cardstock on the bottom. Use the tape to hold them in place.

If you don't like marshmallows, you could use chocolate or cheese, or even compare how long it takes an ice cube to melt inside a solar oven and outside. Put the food you chose to melt on a plate and place it on the black cardstock.

Position the box so it faces the Sun, adjusting the lid so the light is reflected onto the food by the aluminum foil.

Fix the lid at this position with tape or a stick. You might have to move the oven a little as the position of the Sun changes.

You'll need to cover the oven with plastic food wrap to stop the warm air from escaping. It may take over an hour for your food to melt, depending on the temperature and time of day, so be patient!

Only heat up food that doesn't require heating to eat as the solar oven might not get the food to a safe enough temperature for consumption.

⭐ MORE FUN

Try insulating the inside of your solar oven with a material that traps heat. Bubble wrap or newspaper would work well.

⭐ LEARNING POINTS

There are three processes at work in a solar oven. The matte black paper absorbs the heat while solar radiation from the Sun is reflected from the aluminum foil onto the food. The food wrap traps the warm air inside as hot air rises! These three processes together heat up the food, making it melt.

SUN SAFE

✡ SCIENTIFIC CONCEPT—EFFECTS OF ULTRAVIOLET LIGHT

Ultraviolet (UV) light is invisible radiation, which can cause sunburn and damage to your eyes if you don't protect yourself properly. The Earth's atmosphere blocks out a lot of radiation, so the levels in space are much higher than on Earth. Luckily, UV light is fairly easy to block. Astronauts' visors reflect UV light to protect the eyes and face, and the rest of the suit protects the body.

UV beads are perfect for learning about UV radiation. They change color faster and have a deeper color with stronger levels of UV light. UV beads turn back to their original color when the UV light source is removed.

✡ UV beads

✡ String

✡ Paper or cardstock

✡ Sunscreen with different protection factors

Thread a bead on string for each type of sunscreen you want to test, plus one extra for the control, and tie a knot at each end to stop the beads from falling off. This activity is best done on a sunny day, but you could try it on a cloudy day too and compare what happens.

Take the bead string outside and watch what happens. The beads should change color almost instantly.

Lay the string on the paper and assign each bead to a type of sunscreen.

Next, completely cover each bead with the assigned sunscreen and label them on the sheet of paper.

Place the string and paper in the sunshine outdoors and record the color each bead changes. Would you be able to tell which sunscreen was on which bead without knowing? Maybe you could ask a friend if they can guess.

✡ MORE FUN

It might be tricky, but can you half-cover each bead in sunscreen, leaving the other half uncovered so you can see the difference?

✡ LEARNING POINT

Our bodies need UV light to produce vitamin D which strengthens bones and the immune system, but overexposure also causes sunburn and can damage eyes and skin.

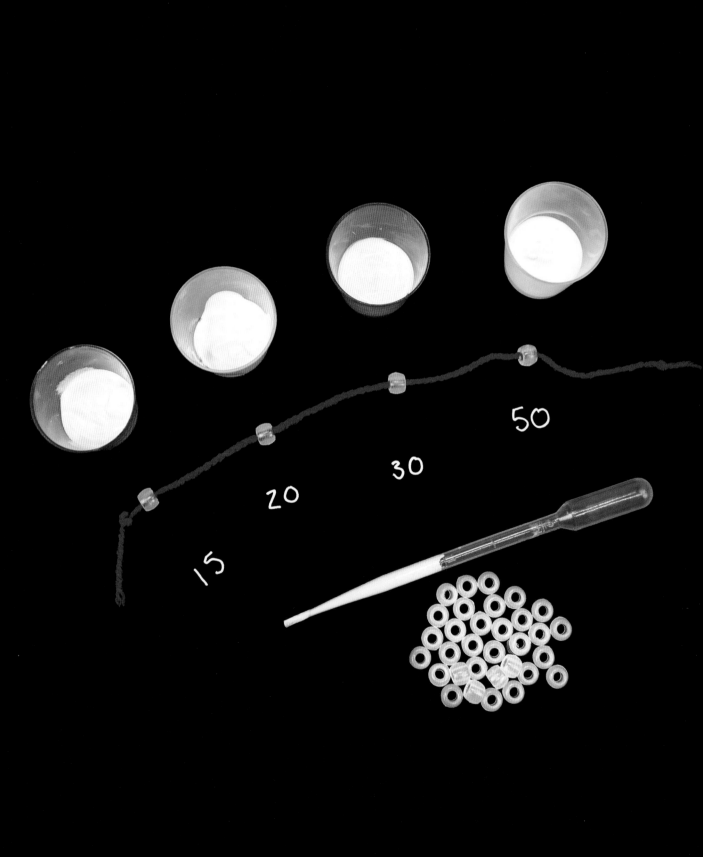

CAN YOU BALANCE?

✡ SCIENTIFIC CONCEPT—EFFECTS OF LIVING IN SPACE ON THE BODY

It takes a bit of time for astronauts to adjust to living in space. Here on Earth, gravity helps us balance, and we have a sense of standing the right way up because the weight of our body is on our feet as we stand on the ground. In space, weightlessness means the brain doesn't have these indicators, leading to astronauts feeling a little nauseated when they first go into space.

✡ Ball

Try to stand on one leg with your arms in the air. Can you balance easily?

Next, try to stand on one leg and throw a small soft ball to a friend also standing on one leg. Can they catch the ball? Is it easier to stand on your right leg or left leg? See if your game of catch is shorter on one leg than two!

✡ MORE FUN

Can you hop and play catch at the same time? How do you think a game of catch would be different on the Moon where there is less gravity?

CLEAN IT UP!

✫ SCIENTIFIC CONCEPT—PROPERTIES OF MATERIALS

Humans need water for survival, but there isn't enough space or weight allowance to take all the water a human would need for a long period in space in a rocket from Earth. The water astronauts drink is cleverly recycled and cleaned, so they can drink the same water over and over again.

One way to clean water is to filter it. Filtering systems in space are very complex, but this easy activity gives you a small insight into the process.

- ✫ Water
- ✫ Glitter, dirt or sand
- ✫ Coffee filter
- ✫ Paper towels
- ✫ Small stones or pebbles
- ✫ Funnel
- ✫ Plastic bottle

Make some dirty water to clean. You can do this by putting a handful of glitter, dirt or sand into the water.

Take a look at the coffee filter, paper towels and stones and think about which will make the best filter.

Once you've decided which to test first, put the material inside a funnel, then put the funnel into an empty plastic bottle before pouring some of your dirty water mixture gently onto the filter. You should find clearer liquid flows through the filter into the bottle below as solid material is trapped on the filter.

Run the same dirty water through the other filters, noting which gives the cleanest water. Is it the one you expected?

Do not drink your filtered water as our drinking water is specially cleaned (not just filtered) to make it safe.

✫ MORE FUN

Try filtering with stones of different sizes. You should find these also trap some of the solid particles in the dirty water, making it look clearer.

✫ LEARNING POINTS

A filter is a material that allows liquid through but traps solid particles, separating solids from liquids.

GROWING TALLER

⚝ SCIENTIFIC CONCEPT—MEASUREMENT

Spending time in space can have serious effects on the human body, as our bodies have adapted to living with gravity on Earth. Living in microgravity for a period of time leads to muscle wastage, changes in blood pressure and bone loss. Imagine spending several months floating instead of walking. The lack of load-bearing exercise can lead to bones becoming weaker, which is why astronauts must exercise for several hours a day in space.

On Earth, the discs that make up our spine are slightly compressed thanks to gravity. In the microgravity of space, that compression no longer happens meaning the discs expand and astronauts become up to 2 inches (5 cm) taller!

⚝ Meter ruler or tape measure

Use a ruler to determine how tall you are on Earth.

Calculate how much taller you could be in space. To do this you'll need to add 2 inches (5 cm) on to your height.

Would being 2 inches (5 cm) taller mean you could do anything more than you can now? Does it make you tall enough to ride a new rollercoaster in a theme park or reach a higher shelf in your kitchen?

⚝ MORE FUN

To reduce the effects of microgravity, astronauts in space exercise daily. Can you devise a fun exercise regime for an astronaut to follow? Weight bearing exercises are best, things like jogging, weight training and dancing, but remember astronauts don't have much space to exercise.

STOP THE FLOATING FOOD!

✡ SCIENTIFIC CONCEPTS—GRAVITY, LIVING IN SPACE

One of the problems astronauts face in space is that the lack of gravity means food floats away. Imagine sprinkling salt or pepper on your food and then watching it float off!

Water or food crumbs floating around a spacecraft could cause serious damage, so it's very important to keep it contained.

Can you design packaging that allows an astronaut to access their food but also stops it from escaping and flying around the spacecraft?

✡ Straws

✡ Food-safe resealable bags

✡ Tape, masking tape, duct tape

✡ Milk or other liquid

One way to create packaging is to use a straw and resealable bag so food can be sucked up. You'll need to make sure you seal the gap around the straw and bag well enough to stop any liquid from escaping.

Carefully make a hole in the side of a resealable bag and push a straw through the hole. Seal around the hole with tape. To test the seal, pour some water in the bag so it's about one-third full, seal the top and tip the bag upside down, covering the end of the straw with your finger. Does any water escape from the bag? If it doesn't, you've got a good seal.

Try adding milk to your food bag to check if you can drink it without any spills.

Can you think of another design to perform the same function? Do any of the different tapes work better than others?

✡ MORE FUN

Imagine an astronaut wants to have a fancy meal while in space. Can you design a way to stop a knife and fork floating around, but still be usable? What other problem might you have?

Hint—how about using a tray and magnets? Would the food still float around?

SPACE CIRCUITS

✭ SCIENTIFIC CONCEPT—ELECTRICITY

The International Space Station is powered by electricity from solar power. Solar arrays convert sunlight into electricity for the Space Station to use. Electricity flows through a circuit, but this only works if the circuit is complete. You can make your own circuits and learn how electricity flows using play dough.

- ✭ Play dough
- ✭ AA battery holder with wire leads and batteries
- ✭ Light emitting diodes (LEDs)
- ✭ Star cookie cutter

To make a simple circuit, roll two pieces of the play dough into balls, and check that the batteries are in the battery holder. Place the red lead into one piece of dough and the black into another. Make sure the two balls of dough are not touching.

Look at the LED: one end is longer than the other. It's important to remember that electricity can flow only one way through an LED. The long leg is the positive leg and should be pushed into the play dough ball with the red wire, while the shorter lead should be in the play dough ball with the black wire.

If the LED is in the play dough the right way, you should find it lights up! Electricity always takes the easiest path, so if you push the two play dough balls together it will flow through the play dough and not the LED . . . meaning the LED won't light up!

Once you've got the hang of how a circuit works, use a cookie cutter to make the play dough star or planet shaped. Can you make a space circuit?

✭ MORE FUN

Can you make a circuit to represent a constellation? Remember, for electricity to flow the circuit must be complete with no breaks.

✭ LEARNING POINTS

Play dough conducts electricity because it contains salt. Salt ions allow electricity to flow through the play dough. If you wanted to make an insulating (nonconducting) play dough, you wouldn't add the salt.

PLAY DOUGH RECIPE

- ✭ ¼ cup (60 g) salt
- ✭ 1 cup (125 g) flour
- ✭ Food coloring
- ✭ ½ cup (120 ml) warm water

Mix the salt with the flour. Mix 4 to 6 drops of food coloring with the water. Add the water to the flour mix and knead by hand until well mixed. Store in a tightly sealed container.

DEHYDRATE IT!

A big problem for astronauts in space is food. There isn't the room or weight allowance on a spacecraft to transport months worth of food, so what is taken must be light and last for a long time.

Some of the first space foods were packaged up like toothpaste in tubes, which astronauts would squeeze into their mouths. They probably didn't taste very nice, so as time spent in space started to increase, scientists wanted to improve food quality.

One way to provide good food, but keep the weight down, is to cook it, freeze it and then remove the water.

You can try dehydrating your own food in an oven, or use the Sun if you live somewhere with strong sunlight.

✬ Food to dehydrate (apples or tomatoes work well)

✬ Baking sheet

Ask a grown-up to help with this activity. To make dried apples, have an adult carefully slice the apple into thin slices and spread them out on a baking sheet. Place the apples in an oven on the lowest setting for 6 to 8 hours. If you want them more crisp like apple chips, use a higher setting, around 350°F (177°C) for about an hour or until they look crisp and slightly brown. Try weighing a couple of apple slices before and after drying to see how much weight you save by drying them.

If it's a sunny day, you can try to dehydrate foods in the Sun. This is especially good for tomatoes. You'll need to thinly slice the tomatoes and place them on a baking sheet in the sunshine. It'll take a few days for the tomatoes to dry out so remember to cover them and bring them in at night.

✬ MORE FUN

Try drying herbs. Give them a good wash, and then bundle them together before hanging them up in the Sun to dry.

✬ LEARNING POINT

Dehydrating food allows it to last a long time at normal temperatures and retain its nutritional value, making it great for astronauts spending a period of time in space.

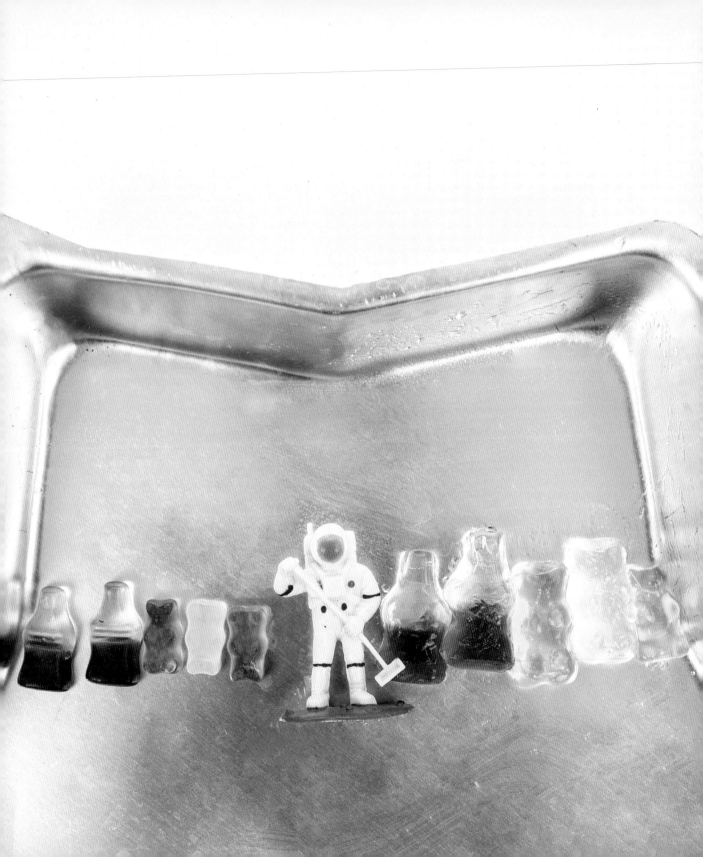

REHYDRATE IT!

All living things need water to survive—without water, your body would stop working properly. If your body doesn't have enough water, you are dehydrated. Severe dehydration can make you feel very poorly.

We've tried dehydrating foods; now it's time to rehydrate them. To rehydrate a food, you need to restore the water. Astronauts use water to rehydrate their food in space.

✬ Cold water

✬ Bowl

✬ Foods to rehydrate (raisins, dried apples; small jelly sweets also work)

Pour the cold water into the bowl and put the dehydrated food in the water. It takes a bit of time for water to be reabsorbed by the food, so be patient and top up with water if the bowl starts to run dry.

You should find the dehydrated food plumps up over a few hours!

Only use clean, cold water to rehydrate your food, unless you're going to boil it before eating.

✬ MORE FUN

In the future, astronauts might be able to grow their own food in space. Try growing cress (greens) or herbs that you can eat at home. Remember plants need to be kept in a cool, light place and watered regularly.

✬ LEARNING POINT

Did you know about 20 percent of our water intake comes from food? Foods like watermelon, celery and cucumber all have a high water content, so are great for helping you stay hydrated.

LANDSCAPED LANDING

For a spacecraft to return to Earth safely it must drastically reduce its speed before touchdown. One way to slow a spacecraft down is to use a parachute. Parachutes create drag, reducing the rocket's speed.

When a spacecraft returns to Earth, it must reenter the Earth's atmosphere. Gravity starts to pull it back to Earth, while the craft hitting and rubbing against air particles at high speed creates friction and air resistance, slowing it down. The slower speed is helpful, but the intense heat created by friction isn't. A spacecraft has to be made of super strong materials that can withstand such high temperatures.

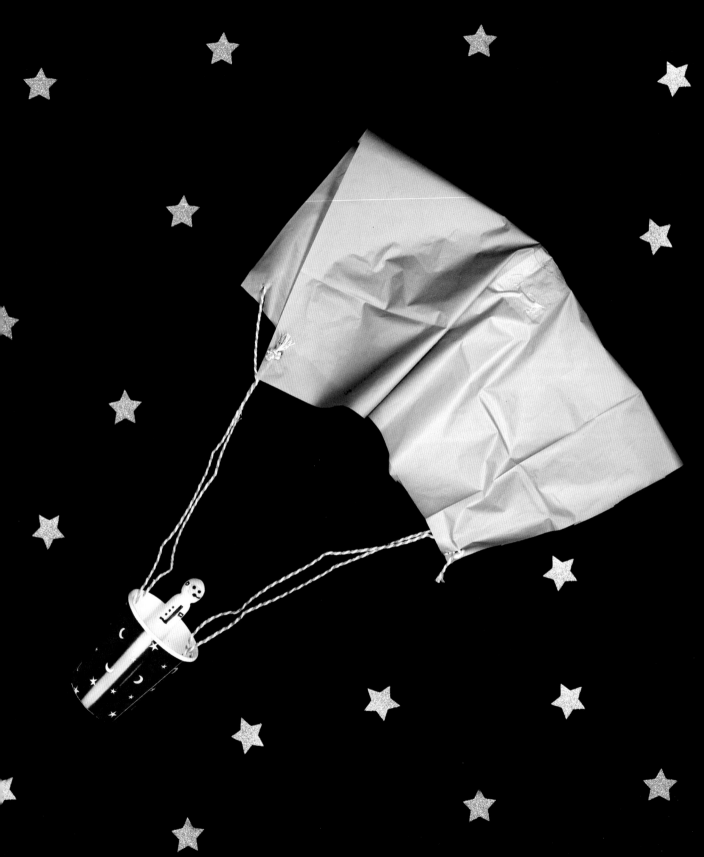

PARACHUTE

☆ SCIENTIFIC CONCEPTS—GRAVITY, AIR RESISTANCE

When objects fall, two forces act on them: gravity pulls the object down, while air resistance slows the fall.

If you drop a piece of paper and a stone at the same time, the stone hits the ground first. This is because there is more air resistance acting on the paper as it has a larger surface area. The paper seems to "catch" the air, which slows it down. The force of gravity acting on both the paper and the stone is the same.

Parachutes are used to slow the fall of an object by increasing air resistance, which reduces the effect of gravity. Rocket capsules use parachutes when they land to use air resistance to slow them down as much as possible.

This activity investigates the relationship between the shape of a parachute and how fast it falls.

- ☆ Cotton or plastic sheet
- ☆ Scissors
- ☆ Tape
- ☆ String
- ☆ Plastic or paper cup
- ☆ Astronaut or toy figure
- ☆ Timer
- ☆ Scales

Cut out the parachute from the cotton sheet. Think carefully about how big you think the parachute should be. The bigger the parachute, the more it will increase air resistance and slow the fall of the astronaut. The parachute could be a square or a circle shape; do you think this will make a difference?

Ask an adult to carefully make 4 holes in the parachute, one in each corner. If using a circle shape, space out the holes evenly.

Cut four lengths of string to the same length and tie one to each hole in the parachute. Attach the other ends evenly to the inside of the paper or plastic cup and secure with tape. Add an astronaut or toy figure.

Hold the parachute above your head and ask a friend to time how long it takes to reach the ground. If you make the parachute bigger, you should find it falls to the ground more slowly.

☆ MORE FUN

Try adding figures of different weights to the parachute and record the time it takes for each to reach the ground.

Can you make a double parachute?

☆ LEARNING POINTS

Have you ever watched a feather or other similarly shaped object, like a leaf or piece of paper, drop to the ground? These fall much more slowly than a small heavy object like a stone. This is because air resistance, or drag, slows the feather down more than the stone.

Imagine swimming through the air with your arms pushing the atmosphere out of your way. Then imagine having a big sheet of cardboard attached to each hand. The cards make the surface area of your hands bigger, and increase the air resistance. It's the same with parachutes. The bigger the parachute, the larger the surface area, the greater the air resistance and the slower the object falls.

DROP IT!

✫ SCIENTIFIC CONCEPTS—GRAVITY, AIR RESISTANCE

If there were no air resistance, a feather and a stone dropped from the same height would hit the ground at the same time. This is because the only force acting on them would be gravity, and the strength of the gravitational force acting on both would be the same.

This activity investigates the relationship between the shape of a parachute and how fast it falls.

✫ 2 small empty water bottles

✫ Sand, water or rice

✫ Weighing scales

✫ Paper

Make sure the water bottles are empty, dry and both the same size.

Fill one bottle about half full with sand. Hold both bottles up as high as you can reach and drop them at the same time. They should both hit the ground at the same time because the force of gravity acting on both is the same. Can you weigh your bottles and see how much heavier one is than the other? Does the weight matter?

Next, try dropping a piece of paper rolled into a ball and one held out flat. The ball of paper will hit the ground first as there is more air pushing up onto the sheet of paper slowing it down. Parachutes use air resistance to slow the fall of the object attached.

✫ MORE FUN

If you make an identical parachute for both your bottles, do you think they will still hit the ground at the same time?

✫ LEARNING POINTS

If a stone and a feather were dropped at the same time on the Moon, they would both hit the ground at the same time. This is because, unlike on Earth, there is no air resistance on the Moon, so both the stone and feather would have only the force of gravity acting on them.

LIFT WITH BALLOONS

☆ SCIENTIFIC CONCEPT—GRAVITY

Have you ever wondered why a helium balloon floats, but a normal balloon filled with air drops to the ground?

Objects float if they are lighter than the air around them. A balloon filled with air will drop to the ground, as it is heavier than air thanks to the weight of the balloon. A balloon filled with helium gas will float, as helium gas is less dense than air.

In order to reach space, a rocket must overcome the downward force of gravity. Of course, this cannot be done with helium balloons, but imagine if it was that easy!

☆ String

☆ Helium-filled balloons

☆ Small toy (a LEGO figure is a good size)

☆ Reusable adhesive putty

Tie the string to the helium balloon, making sure it's long enough for you to reach when you let go of the balloon and it hits the ceiling.

Attach a small toy figure to the string. If the figure stays on the ground when you drop the balloon, add more balloons until the figure lifts into the air.

If the toy figure rises up with just one balloon, try adding adhesive putty to the figure to increase its weight until it drops to the ground again.

☆ MORE FUN

Can you find a point where your toy figure is floating in the air, not being pulled down by gravity or up by the helium balloon?

☆ LEARNING POINTS

Helium is a colorless, tasteless and odorless gas and the second most common element in the universe.

Because helium is lighter than air and chemically unreactive (this means it doesn't react with other chemicals and so is very safe), it's often used to fill balloons and airships.

FEELING THE BURN

✿ SCIENTIFIC CONCEPTS—GRAVITY, FRICTION, RESISTANCE

Reentry into the Earth's atmosphere is a dangerous part of space travel. As a spacecraft falls, it heats up because of friction and air resistance created by air particles hitting the surface of the spacecraft at high speed. The part of a spacecraft which returns to Earth must be protected by heat shields to protect it from the intense heat.

This activity uses black and white paper wrapped around a jar of water to demonstrate the different properties of the two materials.

✿ 3 jars
✿ 1 sheet of black paper
✿ 1 sheet of white paper
✿ 1 sheet of foil paper or aluminum foil
✿ Thermometer

Put the same amount of cold water in each jar. Cover one jar with black paper, one with white and one with foil. Use a thermometer to record the initial temperature.

Leave the jars outside in the sunshine and check their temperature every 5 minutes. You should find that the black paper absorbs heat, and transmits this heat to the jar, heating the water. The heat from the black paper should increase the water temperature more than the white and shiny paper-covered jars, which reflect heat so it doesn't reach the water.

✿ MORE FUN

Next time you go out, think about what color clothes to wear. Do you want to stay cool or keep warm?

✿ LEARNING POINTS

Did you know that some colors absorb more light than others? Dark objects look dark because they absorb light. The light absorbed is transformed into heat energy so dark colors not only absorb light but they emit heat. Have you ever worn a black T-shirt on a warm day and found it made you very hot? It's better to wear a white T-shirt than a black T-shirt on a sunny day because a white T-shirt reflects light, absorbing less heat. Dark colored materials absorb the most light and heat up more than other colors.

SUPER SOLAR SYSTEM

The solar system is made up of the Sun and objects that orbit around it. The solar system has eight planets; Mercury, Venus, Earth and Mars are the inner planets. Beyond Mars there is an asteroid belt and beyond that are four much larger outer planets. These are the gas giants Jupiter, Saturn, Uranus and Neptune. The closest of the gas giants to the Sun is Jupiter, but even Jupiter is so far that light takes 43 minutes to reach it from the Sun, compared with just 8 minutes to reach Earth.

To give you an idea of the sizes involved, 1.3 million Earths would fit inside the Sun and 764 Earths would fit inside Saturn! Neptune, the farthest out of the gas giants, is 30 times farther from the Sun than Earth and takes 165 Earth years to orbit the Sun.

The Kuiper Belt lies on the outskirts of the solar system and contains dwarf planets (including Pluto, Eris and Ceres), asteroids, dust, rocks and ice. These dwarf planets are smaller than our Moon.

It's the pull of gravity from the Sun that keeps planets and other objects in orbit around the Sun rather than flying into space.

IN THE SHADOWS

Space is very, very cold: around –455°F (–270°C). This is because space doesn't have an atmosphere, so there's nothing to trap the heat. However, the opposite can be said for the Sun, whose surface burns at 10,000°F (5,600°C). If you were on the side of the Moon with the Sun shining on you, it would feel very hot, as the Moon has no atmosphere to absorb sunlight.

Light travels in straight lines, but can be reflected, absorbed or scattered depending on the material it comes into contact with. Shadows form when something blocks the path of the light. You can make a shadow puppet to demonstrate this.

✮ Black paper

✮ White paper

✮ Tracing paper

✮ Craft sticks

✮ Double-sided tape

✮ A sunny day or flashlight

Cut out a rocket shape from each of the paper types and attach them to sticks using double-sided tape to make rocket shaped shadow puppets.

If it's a sunny day, take the puppets outside and use them to make shadows on the ground. You should find the darkest shadows form from the black rockets as these don't let any light pass through them. The tracing paper will let some light through, but not all, so the shadow won't be as dark. If it's a cloudy day, use the flashlight to act as the Sun making a shadow against the puppets.

✮ MORE FUN

Can you create a shadow theater and make up a story using the shadow puppets?

✮ LEARNING POINT

Try moving the shadow rockets closer to the ground. This should make the shadows smaller. Shadows will also be smallest at midday when the Sun is highest in the sky.

SPACE CAMP STARGAZING

✨ SCIENTIFIC CONCEPT—ASTRONOMY

You don't need a fancy telescope to see the wonders of the night sky. On a clear night you should be able to see planets, star clusters and if you're very lucky, a shooting star.

✨ Weather appropriate clothing

✨ Blanket

✨ Insect repellent, optional

✨ Binoculars, optional

You'll need a clear night to try stargazing and preferably a place without much light pollution from other sources.

Make sure you're dressed for the weather, grab a blanket and an adult, and see what you can spot.

Don't forget to give your eyes time to get used to the darkness. Can you draw a map of the night sky and keep a diary of what you can see over a period of a few weeks or months?

✨ MORE FUN

How many constellations can you spot? Orion is a good one to start with: Look for the three stars of his belt in a row. Online resources can show you the constellations visible to you based on your location and the time of year.

How about setting up a space camp in your backyard with some friends? You could start the day with a solar oven and finish with some stargazing.

✨ LEARNING POINTS

Astronomy is the study of space, including stars, planets and galaxies.

WALK THE SOLAR SYSTEM

⭐ SCIENTIFIC CONCEPT—MEASUREMENT

Space is mind-blowingly massive. Did you know that more than 1,300 Earths would fit inside Jupiter, and 1.3 million Earths would fit inside the Sun? To walk the solar system requires a huge scale-down of the distances involved, and even then probably needs to be done outside.

Calculating how far each planet is from the Sun is not an easy task, as the distance changes depending where the planet is in its orbit and the numbers involved are so big. Astronomers sometimes use Astronomical Units as a measurement. An AU is the distance from the Earth to the Sun.

⭐ Chalk

To begin, scale down the distances involved to a manageable figure. An easy way to do this is to use a scaling factor.

If we multiply each planet's distance from the Sun in AU by 40 inches (100 cm), you get a distance you can walk, although you might want to stop at Saturn unless you have a large space.

Draw the Sun on the ground using chalk and then use your scaled-down measurements to walk to each planet, making a mark for each one.

⭐ MORE FUN

Try using a different scaling factor. How do the numbers change? Can you still walk the solar system easily?

⭐ LEARNING POINTS

Distances in space are so vast that the measurements we use on Earth don't really work. One AU is about 93 million miles (150 million km)! The Earth is only 24,000 miles (40,000 km) around.

SOLAR SYSTEM DISTANCES

Mercury ⭐ 0.4AU

Venus ⭐ 0.7AU

Earth ⭐ 1.0AU

Mars ⭐ 1.5AU

Asteroid Belt ⭐ 2.8AU

Jupiter ⭐ 5.2AU

Saturn ⭐ 9.6AU

Uranus ⭐ 19.2AU

Neptune ⭐ 30.0AU

Pluto ⭐ 39.5AU

NEWTON'S CRADLE

✦ SCIENTIFIC CONCEPT—CONSERVATION OF ENERGY

A Newton's Cradle is a great way to demonstrate the laws of conservation of energy. We're going to use marbles for the balls, but you could also use wooden beads and paint them to match each planet.

When the first ball of the cradle collides with the second, the first ball stops, but its momentum is transferred to the second ball. The same thing happens with each ball until the last one is reached. You should find that the last ball swings up with the same momentum as the first.

- ✦ Craft sticks, wooden frame or cardboard box
- ✦ Hot glue gun and glue
- ✦ String or thread
- ✦ Scissors
- ✦ 5 marbles of the same size
- ✦ Tape

First, create a frame for the cradle. You could use craft sticks, a wooden frame or even a cardboard box. A length of about 6 inches (15 cm) and height of 4 inches (10 cm) works well.

Use a hot glue gun to stick your frame together securely if using a wooden frame. If you use a cardboard box, cut out the sides, top and bottom, leaving just a frame behind.

Cut 10 pieces of string or thread (2 for each marble). These should all be the same length and the same length as the height of your frame.

Attach two pieces of string or thread to opposite sides of the marble using glue, and leave to dry. Using a hot glue gun is a good way to do this (ask an adult to help).

Hang the marbles one by one from the top edges of the frame with one string taped to the top of the right side and one to the left giving you a triangle shape. Each marble needs to touch the marble/s next to it and be at exactly the same height.

Once the marbles are in place, gently pull up the first marble and let go. This should make the marble at the opposite end move, leaving the center 3 marbles stationary.

✦ MORE FUN

Can you create a bigger version of your cradle?

✦ LEARNING POINTS

While the momentum is transferred between the balls, they won't swing forever as other effects (such as friction) means that the arc of the balls lessens with time and they eventually come to a stop.

FILTER PAPER CHROMATOGRAPHY PLANETS

⭐ SCIENTIFIC CONCEPT—CHROMATOGRAPHY

Chromatography is a technique used to separate mixtures. Did you know the ink in felt tip pens is usually made up of more than one color? We can pass the ink through filter paper to separate the colors out.

As well as being a handy scientific technique, chromatography is great for making colorful pictures, and the way the colors spread and mix is perfect for making planets.

- ⭐ Felt tip pens, selection of washable and permanent
- ⭐ Filter paper discs
- ⭐ Flat tray
- ⭐ Droppers
- ⭐ Water

Think about the colors you need to make for each planet. Mars mostly looks red, while Jupiter is a mixture of yellow, red, brown and white.

Decide which planet to try first and draw lots of different colored dots on a piece of filter paper. Put the filter paper on a waterproof tray and carefully drip a few drops of water onto each colored dot and watch as the colors spread.

You'll need to hang your filter paper up to dry because if you leave it in a wet tray all the color will eventually leach out.

⭐ MORE FUN

Can you use the same technique to make moons for the planets? Which color felt tips could you use for this?

⭐ LEARNING POINTS

Mars was named after the Roman god of war because of its red color. Jupiter's Great Red Spot is a huge storm that has been raging away for hundreds of years.

REVOLVING SOLAR SYSTEM

☆ SCIENTIFIC CONCEPTS—SOLAR SYSTEM, ORBITS

Our solar system is just a small part of the vast expanse of space. All of the planets in our solar system move around the Sun in a path called an orbit. They are held in orbit by gravity. The time taken for each planet to spin once is called a day and the time taken for each to complete one orbit of the Sun is a year. Days and years are different lengths for each planet as they spin at different rates and have different length orbits.

To build a model of the solar system, you'll need colored cardstock cut into planet shapes, strips of black cardstock cut into different lengths, split pins and tape.

☆ Colored cardstock

☆ Black strips of cardstock

☆ Split paper fasteners or cotter pins

☆ Double-sided tape

Decide which planets you're going to include in your model. Are you feeling brave enough to try all of them? Cut out a circle to represent each planet. Think about their size relative to each other. For example, the inner planets are much smaller than the outer planets. Remember we said that 1.3 million Earths would fit inside the Sun and 764 Earths would fit inside Saturn?

You'll also need a cutout of the Sun to go in the center.

Take a small black strip of cardstock and attach one end to the center of your sun with a split pin. Use double-sided tape to attach Mercury to the opposite end. You should be able to move Mercury in orbit around the Sun. Do the same for each planet in order of how far they are from the Sun to build up the model.

☆ MORE FUN

Can you add a Moon to orbit the Earth? It might be hard to add Jupiter's many moons, but you could add two to Mars. Phobos is larger than Deimos and closer to the surface.

☆ LEARNING POINT

It is the powerful pull of gravity from the Sun that keeps planets and other objects in the solar system in orbit around it.

CONSTELLATION DOT-TO-DOTS

✡ SCIENTIFIC CONCEPT—CONSTELLATIONS

A constellation is a group of stars that form a shape and have a name. For example, Ursa Major is in the shape of a bear and the seven brightest stars in the northern sky look a bit like a saucepan. This saucepan is sometimes called the Big Dipper.

We can make constellations using glitter glue or star stickers on black cardstock and then join the dots to see the shape.

✡ Glitter glue pen or star stickers

✡ Black cardstock

✡ Silver pen

Decide which constellation you'd like to create. The Big Dipper, Cepheus and Canis Major are all nice easy shapes.

Use a glitter glue pen or star stickers to mark out each constellation on black cardstock and then connect the stars together using a silver pen.

Create several constellation pictures and ask a friend to try to join the dots and guess what the constellation looks like.

✡ MORE FUN

Can you make a matching card game, where one card is the star shape and one a picture representing the constellation? You could mix up the cards, turn them all over and take turns to find the matching star shape and constellation.

✡ LEARNING POINTS

Constellations are arrangements of stars representing objects, animals and mythical creatures. Different constellations can be seen in the sky throughout the year, and depend on which hemisphere you live in. This is because of the movement of the Earth as it orbits the Sun.

SPACE PROBE

⭐ SCIENTIFIC CONCEPT—SURVIVAL IN SPACE

A space probe is a craft that travels through space gathering information and sending it back to Earth. Space probes can be sent into space to orbit or even land on a planet. Space probes don't have people on them and are not usually designed to return to Earth.

Depending on where it is traveling, a space probe must be able to cope with extreme hot or cold temperatures. Can you design a space probe with features to protect it from the heat or cold?

⭐ Insulating materials (cotton wool, bubble wrap)

⭐ Materials to reflect heat (aluminum foil)

⭐ Cardboard boxes

⭐ Cardboard tubes

For this activity, think about the type of materials that absorb or reflect heat. Remember dark materials absorb light, which is transformed into heat energy, while white materials reflect light and absorb less heat. Can you design a model of a space probe using both insulating and heat-reflecting materials?

Space probes often have solar panels to convert energy from the Sun into electricity as well as a propulsion module and antenna for communication. Can you add these into your design?

If you could choose anywhere in our Solar System, where would you send your probe? If you're sending your probe to a hot planet, think about how you would protect it from the extreme cold of space and high temperatures on the surface of the planet.

⭐ MORE FUN

Think about what a picture of Mars would look like taken from a space probe. Can you draw how you think it would look?

SPIN ART GALAXIES

✩ SCIENTIFIC CONCEPT—GRAVITY, GALAXIES

A galaxy is a gigantic group of stars, gas and dust held together by gravity. Our solar system is part of a spiral-shaped galaxy called the Milky Way. The next nearest galaxy to us is the Andromeda galaxy, which is also a spiral. Lenticular galaxies are flat with a central bulge, elliptical galaxies are round and galaxies with no particular shape are called irregular.

Did you know you can use a salad spinner to create a fun galaxy picture? You'll need some black paper or cardstock, paint and glitter.

✩ Black cardstock or paper

✩ Salad spinner that you no longer need to use for food

✩ Paint

✩ Glitter

Cut the black cardstock to a size that fits neatly inside the salad spinner bowl.

Think about what color you'd like your galaxy picture to be. Squirt paint of those colors onto the card inside the salad spinner. Add a bit of glitter for extra sparkle.

When you're ready to make the spin art, put the lid on the salad spinner and spin for about 30 seconds. Open up the spinner and check the picture. If you think it needs more of a spin, do it again. Try making one picture by spinning the spinner slowly and another by spinning it quickly. What do you notice?

Do your pictures look like any particular type of galaxy?

✩ MORE FUN

Can you mark some constellations on your spin art pictures?

POPPING PLANETS

⚡ SCIENTIFIC CONCEPTS—FORCES, GRAVITY, TRAJECTORY

This fun activity is another demonstration of forces causing motion. If you pull back on the balloon part of the popper and let go, the force of the balloon makes the ping pong balls fly through the air. You can try pulling the balloon farther and farther back to investigate how increasing the force affects the flight of the balls.

⚡ Table tennis balls or pom-poms

⚡ Permanent pens, felt tip pens or paint

⚡ Scissors

⚡ Plastic or paper cup

⚡ Balloon

⚡ Double-sided tape

Decorate the balls to look like planets using the pens. Once you've finished the planets, you need to make the popping device.

Cut the bottom off the cup and then cut the end (not the part you blow into) of a balloon. Tie the end of the balloon you would blow into and push the open end over the bottom of your cup. You might need to use some tape to attach the balloon.

Pop a ball planet or pom-pom inside the shooter, pull back the balloon and watch the planet fly.

Try changing the angle, adding more than one ball and using different amounts of force to see how the flights change.

⚡ MORE FUN

What do you think will happen if you use smaller, lighter balls? Will they travel farther?

⚡ LEARNING POINTS

If you pull back the balloon end farther, the pom-poms or balls should travel farther as a greater force acts to push them forward.

WHERE IS SPACE?

An atmosphere is a mixture of gases surrounding a planet. The atmosphere of the Earth consists mostly of nitrogen and oxygen. It helps protect the Earth from radiation as well as to absorb heat from the Sun, allowing the Earth to maintain a stable temperature. We couldn't survive on Earth without the protection from radiation and sunlight we get from the atmosphere.

There are five layers within the Earth's atmosphere. The Troposphere contains most of the air and oxygen we need to survive, and weather is formed in this layer.

The Exosphere is the final layer of the atmosphere which extends into space.

✡ Honey

✡ Corn syrup

✡ Dish soap

✡ Water

✡ Vegetable oil

✡ Large, narrow jar

✡ Sticky labels

✡ Pen

Pour the substances in the jar one by one in the order they are listed above—honey, corn syrup, dish soap, water and vegetable oil. Remember to pour slowly and carefully. The liquids stack on top of each other because they have different densities.

Try not to let the thicker liquids touch the sides of the jar as they will stick, and it will look messy, but sometimes it helps to pour the thinner liquids down the side so they don't damage the lower layers.

Can you fill the first three layers to scale and label them using the sticky labels? You'll have to adjust this depending on the size of your jar, but $\frac{1}{16}$ inch to 1 mile or 1 mm to 1 km are good starting points.

✡ MORE FUN

Can you find an object to float on each layer?

✡ LEARNING POINTS

Each of the liquids has a different mass of molecules or different numbers of parts squashed into the same volume of liquid. This gives them different densities allowing one to sit on top of the other—the more dense a liquid is the heavier it is.

EARTH'S ATMOSPHERE

Troposphere ✡ 5 to 9 miles (8 to 14.5 km)

Stratosphere ✡ 9 to 31 miles (14.5 to 50 km)

Mesosphere ✡ 31 to 53 miles (50 to 85 km)

Thermosphere ✡ 53 to 372 miles (85 to 600 km)

Exosphere ✡ 372 to 6,200 miles (600 to 10,000 km)

BALLOON-POWERED MOON BUGGY

✡ SCIENTIFIC CONCEPT—NEWTON'S THIRD LAW

The surface of the Moon varies considerably. Some areas are flat, some sloped; there are also rocky areas and lots of craters.

A moon buggy must to be able to cope with tricky terrain to survive on the Moon.

This balloon-powered moon buggy is another example of Newton's Third Law (page 47), as air rushes out of the balloon backward but the reaction force pushes the balloon forward.

✡ Straws

✡ Axles

✡ Wheels (jar lids, CDs)

✡ Something for the body of your car (bottle, cardboard box, sheet of cardstock)

✡ Tape

✡ Small rubber band

✡ Balloon

This balloon can be used to power a small vehicle.

Think how you're going to construct your moon buggy. You'll need a chassis, wheels and axles to start with. Cut two straws so they are about ⅝ inch (15 mm) shorter than the axles and push the axles inside the straws. Attach wheels to the end of each axle. The straw must be able to move freely around the axle.

Cut a piece of cardstock or a cardboard box so it is narrower than the axles and attach them together by taping over the straws.

Once you've built the frame, use a small rubber band to attach a balloon to the end of a straw. You then need to tape the straw to the top of the moon buggy. Blow the balloon up by blowing into the straw, place the buggy on

the floor, let go and watch it move. If it doesn't work, it might be too heavy, so try to make it lighter.

Of course a balloon-powered moon buggy wouldn't work on the Moon, but can you think of another way to power a moon buggy? How about using the power of the Sun?

✡ MORE FUN

Think about what else a moon buggy needs: maybe a scoop to collect samples, seats for the astronauts and strong, tough wheels?

What could you add to the wheels to allow them to move over ice without slipping?

✡ LEARNING POINTS

If you blow up a balloon and let it go, air escapes from the balloon so quickly the balloon flies around until it runs out of air. When you blow into the balloon, you increase the air pressure inside which makes the balloon material stretch outward. If you let go of the balloon without sealing the end, the energy in the stretched balloon (potential energy) forces air out backward but a reaction force pushes the balloon forward.

HOW DENSE?

✡ SCIENTIFIC CONCEPT—DENSITY

Our sun is an average-size, medium-hot star. Stars start their life in a giant cloud of dust, called a nebula. Once a star is formed, it usually burns energy for billions of years. At the end of its life, a star collapses to become a white dwarf star. Larger stars create a huge nuclear explosion called a supernova and then become either a black hole or a neutron star. Neutron stars are tiny, but extremely dense.

This activity shows how different liquids and objects can have different densities.

- ✡ Plastic jar or bottle with a lid
- ✡ Oil
- ✡ Water
- ✡ Food coloring
- ✡ Glitter
- ✡ Pipette

We can learn about several concepts with a density jar. First, think about what will happen when you add oil and water to the jar. Will the two substances mix? Add them both and find out. Try shaking the jar, what happens?

Oil and water don't ever mix, because water is a polar molecule. It has a positive charge on one end and a negative charge on the other. Water molecules are attracted to each other as the positive end of one water molecule is attracted to the negative end of another water molecule. Oil is nonpolar and so not attracted to the water, meaning the two never mix.

The oil rests on top of the water because it is less dense. Can you think of a denser liquid that would sit under the water? How about molasses or honey?

Try adding some food coloring and glitter to the water layer. Using the pipette, can you make a sparkly star in the jar?

✡ MORE FUN

What do you think will happen if you add an effervescent heartburn or vitamin tablet to your density jar?

✡ LEARNING POINTS

Density refers to how much mass there is in a space. Imagine an empty drawer. If you add five T-shirts the drawer has a certain density, if you add another five T-shirts the density of the drawer increases because the mass has increased but the size of the space in the drawer (volume) has stayed the same.

PLAY DOUGH EARTH LAYERS

✡ SCIENTIFIC CONCEPT—LAYERS OF THE EARTH

Did you know that at the center of the Earth (inner core) is a huge, incredibly hot metal ball? It's made up mostly of iron and is solid only because of the massive amount of pressure the outer layers place on it.

The outer core is liquid and also made of metals. It's this layer that creates the Earth's magnetic field.

The lower mantle is made of rock. It's so hot that the rock should be molten, but like the inner core, the immense amount of pressure makes it solid.

The upper mantle is made of both solid and liquid rock. It becomes less liquid closer to the surface of the Earth where the temperature is cooler.

The crust of the Earth is the top and thinnest layer. Continental crust refers to land and oceanic crust is below the ocean.

✡ Five different colors of play dough (page 95)

✡ Marble or other small ball

Your challenge is to create a model of the 5 layers of the Earth using play dough and a marble or small ball. The easiest way to do this is to use a ball for the inner core and build the layers around it.

Once you've finished, cut a section out so all the layers can be seen.

✡ MORE FUN

Can you do the same for one of the other inner planets?

MERCURY AND MAGNETS

☆ SCIENTIFIC CONCEPTS—MAGNETISM, HOW CRATERS FORM

Mercury is the closest planet to the Sun and the smallest planet in our solar system.

Mercury spins very slowly, so although it is the closest planet to the Sun, the side facing away from the Sun is very cold. It also has no atmosphere to retain heat and no water, making it very unfriendly for humans.

Like the Earth, Mercury has a magnetic field, although it is much weaker than that of the Earth.

☆ 10 small squares of felt

☆ 2 strong magnets

Magnets attract other magnets and some metals (iron and metals which contain iron). The area over which they attract each other is called a magnetic field. You can test to see how strong a magnet's magnetic field is by putting objects between two magnets.

Start by putting one felt square between two magnets— the magnets are probably still attracted to each other. Keep adding the squares of felt one by one until the magnets no longer attract each other.

☆ MORE FUN

Mercury is also covered in craters. Try dropping different size balls into a small layer of sand from different heights to see how the crater size differs.

MARS AND ITS MOONS

✰ SCIENTIFIC CONCEPT—MARS

Mars has two small moons called Phobos and Deimos. Both are odd, irregular shapes that look more like asteroids than a moon. Phobos is the closest to Mars and shaped a bit like a potato; it's very dark and covered in craters.

✰ Red, gray and black play dough (recipe on page 95)

Use the play dough to create a model of Mars and its two moons. Remember, Phobos is about five times the mass of Deimos, and both have a lot of craters.

✰ MORE FUN

Can you make a list of the things you'd need for a trip to Mars? Remember, Mars has a very thin atmosphere and almost all the air is carbon dioxide, so don't forget to take your own oxygen! It's also very cold, so pack a big, thick coat!

✰ LEARNING POINTS

Mars is the only one of the inner planets to have more than one moon. Phobos and Deimos are the sons of the Greek god of war Ares, who was known as Mars to the Romans.

OLYMPUS MONS

✡ SCIENTIFIC CONCEPT—VOLCANOES

Mars is the fourth planet from the Sun and the second smallest. It can be seen from the Earth as a small, red, disc.

Did you know Mars is home to the biggest planetary volcano in our solar system? Olympus Mons is almost three times as tall as Mount Everest!

Olympus Mons hasn't erupted in millions of years, but you can make your own eruption using a couple of household ingredients.

- ✡ Small empty container or water bottle
- ✡ Sand and small stones
- ✡ Plastic wrap, optional, but does save the sand from getting too messy
- ✡ 2 tsp (8.5 g) baking soda (bicarbonate of soda)
- ✡ 1 tsp dish soap
- ✡ A few drops of red and yellow food coloring
- ✡ 2 tbsp (30 ml) vinegar

Make a volcano shape around the water bottle using the sand and stones. Olympus Mons is a shield volcano, which means it was created by lava flowing slowly down the sides, giving it a short, squat appearance. Carefully build up a volcano shape around your water bottle; it should be slightly sloping like Olympus Mons. If you want to really make your volcano look like Olympus Mons, mold a cliff around the outer edge.

If you want to erupt the volcano more than a couple of times without it going soggy, you can cover it with plastic wrap.

For the eruption, first add the baking soda, dish soap and food coloring to the water bottle. When you're ready, pour in the vinegar and watch the lava flow. If it's a bit slow, add some more dish soap and vinegar, or give it a good stir.

✡ MORE FUN

Olympus Mons has several collapsed craters at its summit, which stretches a massive 50 miles (80 km) across. Give your sand and stone volcano a flat summit and watch how your lava flows over it.

✡ LEARNING POINTS

Vinegar (an acid) and bicarbonate of soda (an alkali) react together to neutralize each other. This reaction releases carbon dioxide which creates bubbles. These bubbles make the dish soap foam up to give the appearance of lava erupting from a volcano.

RED MARTIAN SAND

✪ SCIENTIFIC CONCEPT—CHEMICAL REACTIONS

Most of the surface of Mars is a hot, rocky, dusty desert with canyons, craters, plains and volcanoes. When you look at a photo of Mars, the ground looks red. This is because of iron in the soil rusting.

This activity investigates the conditions needed for metals to rust. Good metals to test are iron and steel, which do rust. Aluminum isn't a good metal to test as it doesn't rust easily (it's coated in aluminum oxide which protects it from corrosion).

✪ Iron nails (bright, not galvanized)

✪ Test tubes or small containers

✪ Steel paper clips

✪ Steel paper clip covered in plastic, or steel wool

✪ Water

✪ Vegetable oil

You can design this investigation in lots of different ways, but sample test conditions could be:

Iron nail in air

Iron nail fully submerged in water

Iron nail half in water

Iron nail fully submerged in water with a coating of vegetable oil on the top (this stops air getting to the nail).

Label the test tubes or small containers for each condition you want to test. Place a nail into each test tube and add water and vegetable oil for the conditions where they are needed.

Each condition can be repeated using a steel paper clip and/or a paper clip covered in plastic.

Once you've set up your conditions, watch how they change over a few days noting down if and when each starts to rust.

✪ MORE FUN

To add an extra condition to your investigation, add salt to water and compare this to water alone. You should find that salt speeds up the rusting process.

✪ LEARNING POINTS

Rust is formed when iron comes into contact with water and oxygen. When iron reacts with oxygen it forms iron oxide which we call rust. This is an example of an irreversible reaction, which means it's a permanent change. It can't be reversed.

GIVE SATURN A BATH

✡ SCIENTIFIC CONCEPT—DENSITY

Saturn is the second largest planet in our solar system, but it's less dense than water, which means it would float if we had a tub of water big enough! Can you imagine a giant planet floating in an even more gigantic bathtub of water?

If something is buoyant, it floats in water. For this activity, you'll need a ball that floats and a ball that sinks. For an object to float, it must be less dense than the water.

✡ Different balls to test

✡ Tub of water

✡ Bubble wrap

Check that you have a ball that sinks and one that floats by testing your balls to see if they float in your tub of water.

Wrap a layer of bubble wrap around the ball that sinks; does it float? If it doesn't float add another layer and try again.

✡ MORE FUN

Lemons float on water—how do you think you could get a lemon to sink?

Hint—try removing the skin. Like bubble wrap, lemon skin is full of air, which reduces the density of the lemon, allowing it float.

Can you think of any other fruits with the same type of skin?

✡ LEARNING POINTS

The bubble wrap makes the ball weigh a little more, but also displaces more water making the ball more buoyant. Bubble wrap is full of air pockets, meaning that it isn't very dense. The bubble wrap and ball together are less dense than the water and so float.

LAVA FLOWS ON VENUS

✩ SCIENTIFIC CONCEPT—VISCOSITY

Venus is the hottest planet in the solar system because its very dense atmosphere traps heat. Venus also has lots of volcanoes and much of the surface is covered with lava flows. Did you know the surface of Venus is covered with strange-shaped structures formed from solidified lava?

How far and fast a lava flow travels depends on its viscosity. High-viscosity lava will flow slowly and only cover a small area, whereas low-viscosity lava flows faster and can cover a much bigger area.

This activity investigates the viscosity of different liquids. Which do you think will travel faster, water or honey? Why do you think this is?

- ✩ A small or large ramp (this could be a cutting board, mini white board or large sheet of cardboard)
- ✩ Box or books to hold the ramp in place
- ✩ Pen and paper
- ✩ Substances to test (ketchup, honey, sugar syrup, water, ice cream syrup)
- ✩ Small containers
- ✩ Timer

A viscosity race can get a little sticky so it might be handy to have some warm water and a towel nearby to wash little hands.

Set up your ramp by leaning it against a box or stack of books—think about how steep you want it to be. You don't want the liquids to flow too fast or too slowly, and remember they should all be tested with the ramp at the same slope.

Draw a start and finish line on your ramp; you're going to time how long each liquid takes to travel between the two lines. Which liquid do you think will be fastest (least viscous)? Why do you think this is?

Pour the same amount of each liquid into a small container and get ready to test them. If you have enough helpers you could start all the liquids off at the same time, or test one at a time.

Pour each liquid onto the ramp at the start line and start the timer. Remember to record the time when each reaches the finish line.

Which liquid is the most viscous? Was it the one you expected?

✩ MORE FUN

How could you make a viscous liquid less viscous? Think about what you could add to it to make it flow more easily.

✩ LEARNING POINTS

Viscosity is a measure of a fluid's resistance to flow. Thicker liquids have a higher viscosity as there is a lot of internal friction, which slows down the flow of the liquid as it moves. The viscosity of lava depends on its temperature and chemical content.

STORMY JUPITER

⚝ SCIENTIFIC CONCEPT—WEATHER

Jupiter is a huge gas giant, made up mostly of hydrogen and helium gases. Did you know Jupiter is so big that all the other planets in the solar system could fit inside it?

If you have seen a picture of Jupiter, you probably noticed its Great Red Spot, which is actually a huge storm about 25,000 miles (40,000 km) wide.

You can easily create a model of a storm using just an empty bottle, water, dish soap and glitter.

⚝ Jar or empty water bottle with a lid
⚝ Water
⚝ Dish soap
⚝ Glitter

This super simple model of a storm looks really impressive. All you need to do is fill your jar almost up to the top with water and squirt in some dish soap and a little glitter.

Remember to replace the lid tightly and then swirl the jar around in a circular motion for a few seconds. When you stop, you should see a storm inside the jar! You can do this again and again once the storm settles.

⚝ MORE FUN

Can you find an object small and light enough to swirl around your storm?

⚝ LEARNING POINTS

When the jar is swirled the liquid inside forms a circular motion, called a vortex, which looks like a tornado.

WINDY NEPTUNE

✭ SCIENTIFIC CONCEPT—WIND, WEATHER

Neptune is a dark, cold gas giant with wild winds that can reach up to 1,500 miles (2,414 km) per hour, making them the strongest in the solar system.

Here on Earth a windsock (a bit like a kite) can be used to work out which way wind is blowing. If there were a windsock on Neptune, it would be flying around in all directions.

You can easily make a windsock using a paper cup and ribbons.

✭ Ribbons of different colors and sizes

✭ Paper cup

✭ Scissors

✭ Double-sided tape

✭ Tape

A windsock is a great way to see how air moves in the wind. First you need to think about how to attach the ribbons to the paper cup. You could make holes and tie the ribbons to the cup (ask an adult to help), or place double-sided tape inside the cup edge and attach ribbons to that.

Once you've decided how to attach your ribbons, spread them out along the inside edge of the cup. The ribbons should be long enough to blow easily in the wind. You'll need to attach an extra ribbon to the top of the windsock so you can hold it or attach it to something outside. To do this, carefully make a hole in the bottom part of the cup (ask an adult to help), then thread a piece of ribbon through the hole and tape it securely to the inside.

If it's a windy day, tie your windsock up outside and watch the ribbons blow around. If it's not windy, try running around with your windsock; you should find that the ribbons wave around in the wind. Can you tell which way the wind is blowing by looking at the windsock?

✭ MORE FUN

Make a paper airplane with wide wings so they catch the wind. Try throwing it outside. What happens?

ROLLING URANUS

⚝ SCIENTIFIC CONCEPT—THE UNUSUAL ORIENTATION OF URANUS

Uranus is a bitterly cold, windy planet, with many moons and faint rings. Uranus is unusual as it's tilted on its side. The Earth is slightly tilted but not nearly as much as Uranus. Imagine Uranus rolling like a ball as it orbits the Sun while the other planets spin like spinning tops. This means Uranus's north and south poles alternate between direct sunlight and complete darkness.

Uranus is slightly larger than Neptune, but smaller in mass. It looks to be a green-blue color because there is a lot of methane gas in the atmosphere.

This activity demonstrates the unusual spin of Uranus.

⚝ Modeling clay

⚝ Skewers

First you need to make your planets and the Sun. Use yellow clay for the Sun, green for Uranus and then pick another planet to model. It doesn't matter which you choose as only Uranus spins on its side.

Think about how big each planet should be. Remember Uranus is one of the giant planets, so if you choose to model one of the inner planets they will be much smaller if you want to make them very slightly to scale.

Once you're happy with your planets, carefully place a skewer into each one. Use the skewer to make your second planet rotate around. Remember the time it takes a planet to make one complete rotation is a day and the time taken to orbit around the Sun is a year.

Think how you can model the spin of Uranus. Try turning the skewer onto its side.

⚝ MORE FUN

Try adding other planets to your model—can you place them in order around the Sun on a piece of black cardstock?

STATIC ELECTRICITY ROCKETS

✰ SCIENTIFIC CONCEPT—STATIC ELECTRICITY

Have you ever rubbed a balloon on your hair and watched your hair stand up on end?

When you rub a balloon on your hair or a woolly sweater, the balloon becomes charged with static electricity. This is an electric charge created when some materials are rubbed together.

You can use static electricity to make tissue paper jump up to a balloon.

Do you think it matters how big your tissue paper rockets are? Do you think bigger or smaller rockets will jump the highest?

✰ Tissue paper

✰ Scissors

✰ Balloon

First you need to make your rockets. Cut several different size rocket shapes from the tissue paper. You're going to investigate which jump up to your balloon most easily.

Blow up a balloon and give it a good rub on your hair or a wooly sweater. If you use your hair, you should find it starts to stick up on end as the balloon becomes charged with static electricity and starts to attract your hair.

Hold the balloon over your tissue paper rockets and watch them jump up towards the balloon. If you hold the balloon close to the rockets, they should stick to the surface of the balloon. Tissue paper is so light that it jumps up to the balloon easily. Do you think other types of paper would do the same? Can you design an investigation to find out?

*See photo on page 108.

✰ MORE FUN

How many balloons can you get to stick to a wall (or yourself) at the same time?

Try rubbing a balloon on different types of fabrics. You should find that wool and synthetic fabrics create static electricity most easily.

✰ LEARNING POINTS

Atoms are made up of a positively charged nucleus with negatively charged electrons in orbit around it. When objects touch, electrons sometimes jump between them, leaving the object that has lost electrons with a positive charge and the object that has gained electrons with a negative charge. In this case, the balloon gains extra electrons causing a buildup of negative charges, or static electricity. It is the static electricity that pulls on the tissue paper rockets, lifting them into the air and onto the balloon.

ROCKETS ON ICE

✡ SCIENTIFIC CONCEPT—FRICTION

Pluto was once thought to be the ninth planet in our solar system, but has since been reclassified as a dwarf planet. Dwarf planets still orbit the Sun but are too small to be planets.

Pluto is a rocky ice planet about 50 times farther from the Sun than Earth, meaning it's incredibly cold. Sunlight takes around 5 hours to reach Pluto, compared to about 8 minutes to reach Earth.

If humans were ever to travel to Pluto, we'd need a form of transport that could move over vast amounts of ice. For a vehicle to move quickly and easily over ice there needs to not be much friction.

- ✡ Water
- ✡ Baking tray
- ✡ Felt, bubble wrap, paper and cellophane
- ✡ Double-sided tape
- ✡ Milk bottle tops
- ✡ Straws

You can make a sheet of ice by putting about ⅜ inch (1 cm) of water into baking tray and placing it in a freezer. Once it's frozen, you need to make your rockets to test.

Cut rocket shapes out of the felt, bubble wrap, paper and cellophane. Use double-sided tape to attach a milk bottle top to one side of each rocket. Place the rockets with the milk bottle top facing upwards on the sheet of ice in a row. Try blowing through a straw towards the milk bottle top on each rocket; you should find that the rockets with rougher surfaces are harder to move as there is more friction between the rocket and the ice.

If you wanted a vehicle to grip ice better and not slip, you'd want it to have wheels with a rough surface to increase the amount of friction. If you want it to slide, you'd want a smooth surface.

✡ MORE FUN

Another way to increase friction between vehicles and ice is to add stone, sand and salt to the surface of the ice. Try spreading a thin layer of sand and salt over your ice sheet; you should find it becomes harder to move the rockets. The salt will also make the ice melt.

Salt makes ice melt by lowering the freezing point of water.

✡ LEARNING POINTS

Friction is the force that slows objects down when they rub against each other. Remember friction is stronger on rough surfaces than smooth surfaces. See page 27.

RESOURCES

SCIENCE BOB STORE
www.sciencebobstore.com
Film canisters, filter paper, UV beads

CAROLINA BIOLOGICAL SUPPLY
www.carolina.com
Syringes, filter paper, UV beads

HOME SCIENCE TOOLS
www.homesciencetools.com
Battery packs, LEDs, syringes, filter paper, UV beads

CONSTELLATION MAP APPS
SkyView Free, Android and iOS
Night Sky, iOS, Night Sky Lite, Android

NATIONAL AERONAUTICS AND SPACE ADMINISTRATION (NASA)
www.nasa.gov
Photographs of planets, constellation maps, educational materials

ACKNOWLEDGMENTS

First, I'd like to give a huge thank you to my incredibly patient husband who frequently comes home to a paint splattered backyard or kitchen table covered in play dough, and who supports and encourages me in everything I do.

My children inspire and motivate me daily with their boundless energy, creativity and endless questions. They have been involved with every activity in this book, from thinking of ideas to patiently helping photograph the final activity. I couldn't have done it without them.

Thank you to all my lovely supportive blogging friends, especially Maggy, Cerys and Anna, who have helped me grow Science Sparks from a tiny blog to a website with a worldwide audience. A big thank you to Lynne and Toby whose encouragement and enthusiasm meant more than they will ever know.

A huge thank you to Page Street Publishing Co. for guiding me through the book-writing process and Charlotte Dart for bringing the activities to life with her awesome photos.

Finally, a big thank you as always to Kerry, without whom Science Sparks would not exist, and who I miss every day.

ABOUT THE AUTHOR

I have loved science for as long as I can remember. As a child, I spent many happy summers making baking soda and vinegar volcanoes, catapults and solar ovens with my little brother.

As a teenager, science subjects were always my favorite and led to me studying Microbiology and Virology at university. I knew when I had my own children that I wanted to encourage them to share my passion for science. Taking the time to sit down together and plan a science activity is an incredibly rewarding way to spend a day. Each child brings their own unique take on whatever we are doing so it's never the same. My children continually surprise me with their creativity, curiosity and sense of wonderment.

I took a break from my career in IT after the birth of my third child and started to blog about our science activities, which eventually led to the creation of www.science-sparks.com. The activities are mostly inspired by books we read and genuine questions the children ask as we go about our day. We have a huge amount of fun as a family learning and creating together. Science has become a hugely enriching and invaluable part of our family life.

I've spent a lot of time over the last 7 years volunteering in schools testing out our investigations and ideas, organizing science afternoons and running science clubs. It's tremendously rewarding and inspiring to see how differently children respond to the same activity, how one question leads to another and generally how much fun they have while learning.

INDEX